Turn Left At Mont Blanc

Turn Left At Mont Blanc

Book One in the Alpine Thru-Hiking series

Dan Colegate

Copyright © 2019 Dan Colegate

If you enjoy this book, please leave a review.

Thank you for your support

Find out more at

www.estheranddan.com

www.instagram.com/estheranddan

www.facebook.com/estheranddan

Contents

1. The Idea

Excited to be setting off on a new adventure and relieved that the previous few months of stress and arguments had finally come to an end. These were my overriding emotions as our lumpy rucksacks, stuffed to the brim with hiking gear, food and an assortment of other stuff we hadn't been able to make our minds up about, vanished into the void of Heathrow Airport luggage handling. All being well Esther and I would be reunited with them in just a few hours' time in Geneva. What came next, we still weren't entirely sure. We didn't have anything we could realistically call a 'plan', just a vague idea and the sense that we had some unfinished business to take care of.

Two and half years earlier, in January 2014, we had been counting down the weeks until we got married, left our jobs behind and embarked on a 2300 kilometre hiking adventure. The trail we'd planned to follow is called the GR5, which extends all the way from the North Sea near The Hague in Holland, to the Mediterranean Sea close to Nice in France! Along this mighty length the GR5 weaves in and out of five countries and includes around 700 kilometres through the high French Alps. We'd always done a fair amount of single day hiking in the UK, mostly in the Lake District, and even hiked for a week along the French Pyrenean Way once upon a time, but we'd never attempted anything remotely like this before. Allowing for the occasional rest day and detour we expected it would take us somewhere between four and five months to cover the distance, so this was a serious bit of hiking we had in the pipeline.

There were a handful of supposedly good reasons for this seemingly hare-brained scheme. Our grand hiking adventure was supposed to be much more than a jolly holiday. Our vision was that it would be an extended honeymoon, a career break, a fresh start in our relationship and a big life reset all rolled into one. Our notice periods at work were due to end in mid-February, a week later we would say our personalised wedding vows in front of our friends and family and then, in the first week of March, we'd start the long walk south. We didn't know exactly what we would find out there on the trail, but we did hope and expect that by the time we were finished we'd be closer as a couple and know just what it was that we wanted to do with our lives, something we felt we'd lost sight of a long time ago.

In contrast to the unemployed nomads we were about to become, during the preceding years Esther and I had always done our best to be 'high-fliers', scrambling up the ladder of success. We'd met at Oxford University, the first in our families to go to university at all, and both left with first class degrees to do further study at Durham University. Research jobs at Cambridge University followed and then, just a short while later, we'd left academia to start our own venture capital backed business. Black tie dinners, young entrepreneur awards and invited presentations, where everyone seemed to want to tell us how well we were doing, filled the next few years. Bigger, faster, better and wealthier seemed to be the goal of everyone around us and it was intoxicating. We decided to dabble in property as well, persuading the bank to lend us more money than they ever should have. From the outside looking in we were definitely climbing the rungs, living a life far removed from that of our childhoods.

The view from the coal face was very different. We barely slept, we fretted about the amount of money we owed, we were continuously under pressure to meet more and more deadlines and there was a complete absence of romance between us. We'd become almost solely business rather than life partners. We talked jargon and spiel at work and then bought the bullshit home with us as well. We

2

turned to comfort eating, grew love handles and lost touch with family and friends. Eventually the fast-paced, start-up culture had invaded pretty much every aspect of our lives with few immediate rewards. Sure, we had decent money coming in but it was all going straight back out again to cover debts. We were like jugglers with too many balls in the air. If we dropped one then the whole show would be over.

But then, that's what adult life was all about, wasn't it? One day it would all pay off. It had to. As my dad, a hard-working veteran of numerous driving and delivery jobs, liked to say, "if it was fun son, they wouldn't call it work".

After a few painful years our business eventually folded and we had to sell most of our property to get rid of much of our debt. Most of our effort, in the end, had come to nought. Our rewritten CV's proclaimed the many constructive lessons we'd learned as a result, but in truth we both felt broken afterwards. Esther retrained to become a personal trainer and I became a Business Development Manager at another university, sitting at a desk assessing possible inventions and trying to get the half-decent ones out into the wider world.

At first it was a relief to have a change, slow down and enjoy a slightly simplified life, but the novelty soon wore off. University administration, it sometimes seemed to me, was an ideal place for someone who wanted to kill off a couple of decades until retirement. My colleagues seemed so hard-working, that they cared so much about their work, while I mostly felt I was drowning in policy documents and red tape. For Esther it was the endless early starts, late nights and long, lonely miles driving between clients in the rain that wore her down. We both had more time off than before, but rarely at the same times of day. What had happened to our dreams? We couldn't even remember what they used to be. The last career dream I could recall was

wanting to be a plumber when I was seven years old. Or
was it an astronaut?

It was against this backdrop of disillusion verging on
depression, combined with a series of health-related
obstacles, that we'd hatched our cunning plan. Spurred on
by movies like "The Way" and books like "The Long Walk
to Jerusalem" that proclaimed the healing and deep insights
that could be achieved on a pilgrimage, we decided we'd put
our lives on hold and go for a long walk instead. The actual
route was a bit of an afterthought. We only chose the GR5
because it started a few kilometres from where Esther's
grandma lived in Holland and it ended with a stretch of
mountains. We liked mountains. We studied the route,
downloaded GPS coordinates, read books and blogs about
ultralight hiking kit, accumulated gear and prepared
resupply boxes for family to post to us every two or three
weeks. Alongside planning a wedding, it was a big job, but
we thought it was coming together.

Then, just weeks before we'd been due to set off, all
of our plans came off the rails because I got a hernia. It
sounds so trivial, so commonplace, but the timing couldn't
have been worse and the way events developed threw
everything into disarray. This particular hole in my
abdominal muscles turned out to be a relic of a bowel-
related surgery I'd had a few years earlier, something I'd
tried to forget about. Now, without any pain or signs of
damage beforehand, an incision in my abdominal muscles
had suddenly re-opened and left my intestines pushing on
my skin from the inside. I looked down one day after a
shower to discover an ugly pink molehill keeping my belly
button company. We knew immediately that there was no
way I could carry a heavy pack until it was fixed, because it
could just rip open even more. We thought we'd struck
lucky when I got offered, and gratefully accepted, a last-
minute NHS surgery slot to repair it, but within a week I
was back in hospital with a serious post-op' infection, which
took a much more serious surgery and three months to

recover from. All of our hiking plans had to be cancelled along with our wedding, which I wasn't well enough to attend.

Still, every cloud has a silver lining! The upshot of all that upheaval was an adventure that was way better than our original plan. My various, still healing, surgery wounds meant that long distance hiking was ruled out for at least another twelve months and so instead we made a snap decision to buy an old motorhome. We found good tenants for our remaining house and apartment, put our lives in the UK into boxes in a friend's attic, and set off for what turned into a two year motorhome adventure through Europe. Keeping costs lower than we thought possible beforehand, and living off a combination of savings and rental income, we relished a return to a genuinely simpler way of life. It turned into a beautiful journey that was as much about emotional healing and reconnecting as a couple as it was about seeking out stunning scenery, although we did lots of that too.

By the end of our second year on the road our outlook on life had changed. A lot! Climbing the ladder of success for the sake of it no longer floated our boats. In the past we'd had a three-year plan, a five-year plan and a ten-year plan, all mapped out in spreadsheets. Now we often woke up not knowing where we'd sleep that night. Life on the road still created plenty of challenges but they usually related to things we could touch, not intangible concepts like stock prices, interest rates and market forces.

Finally, after all those years of scrambling for more, we'd seen just how little we actually needed to be happy. After two years living as nomads we'd felt it was time to let go of the past once and for all. At Easter 2016 we'd returned to the UK to oversee the sale of our Durham apartment and give away ninety percent of the possessions we'd left in storage. We didn't like the idea of having more than one property any more, plus a heap of stuff mouldering away when other people could be using it. We'd once met a cycle tourist in the Lake District who had proudly told us that all of his worldly possessions fitted into just ten removal boxes. We liked the sound of that.

At first we'd expected we'd only have to stay in the UK for a few weeks, but somehow it turned into four months. They were good months for the most part. We saw old friends, had fun visiting places we used to enjoy together and generally revelled in having a place larger than a garden shed on wheels to live in for a little while. But we did still feel a bit trapped. The flat sale seemed to keep stalling and finding new homes for our old stuff, since it was very important to us that things didn't just end up in landfill, was emotionally harder than we'd expected. This was especially true during the 4 weeks we spent helping Esther's parents clear out as well. Turned out their attic contained almost every single teddy, trinket, drawing, sticker, badge and board game from Esther's childhood, each of which we photographed and carefully rehomed. Not that I'm complaining I should add because, when it was done, it felt truly awesome not to be technically responsible for so much accumulated, unseen paraphernalia anymore. Even our steps felt lighter. Still, by the time we finally handed over our apartment keys and loaded the sum total of our remaining things (about fifteen boxes worth) into the back of a small hired van it was mid-July and we weren't quite sure where the previous months had gone.

Renting a van had also not been part our original plan. We'd always assumed that when the time came to leave Durham again we'd simply load what was left of our stuff straight into our own motorhome and hit the road again. The problem was that by July we didn't actually own a motorhome anymore. Towards the end of our second year of travel, for various reasons, we'd been feeling like a change of van. As result, while driving back to the UK at Easter, we'd listed our trusted steed "Homer" on eBay. We'd assumed it would take a while to find a buyer, but alarmingly, within just a week of rolling off the ferry, she had gone for the full asking price. We'd been happily relying on bikes and the occasional hire car ever since and, although we'd occasionally done some web searching for another one, somehow we'd never quite gotten around to committing, an oversight that was suddenly a lot more inconvenient.

Unfortunately, since selling Homer, the number of motorhomes available for sale seemed to have plummeted while the cost had spiked upwards. We did like the look of a couple of 'ex-rental' motorhomes being advertised as "available in November" and which seemed much better value, but that was still four months away. Not much help in our immediate predicament. We couldn't live with family for that long and besides, it was summer and the mountains were calling. Summer in the mountains had provided the highlights of our motorhome adventure and we felt a powerful urge to get back, especially after the previous four months spent faffing around in attics and rummaging through dusty boxes.

Just one week later, on the 20th July, we were at Heathrow airport waving a temporary farewell to our hiking gear. It wasn't the full GR5 we were thinking of doing this time though, 'only' the Alpine section between Geneva and Nice, a paltry 700 kilometres with up to 40,000 metres of climbing that we had given ourselves a month to complete. We could have taken longer, except we had also made a snap decision to splash out some of the money from our apartment sale on a package tour to Egypt in late August, a place both of us had often daydreamed about visiting. In practice this meant that we had until 21st August to get the walk done. The guidebook we'd bought two and a half years earlier suggested that this mountainous portion of the GR5 was possible in 31 days, so we had just enough time. Probably.

Never mind that we hadn't done any hiking for almost a year and hadn't carried a fully laden pack containing a tent and cooking gear for much longer. Never mind that we hadn't studied the route details and bought any local maps. Never mind that we hadn't even seen our tent for years. Surely hiking and camping was like riding a bike. You never forget. Do you?

And besides, we didn't 'have' to hike the GR5. Maybe we'd just backpack around on buses and trains instead? Or maybe make our way over to some other, shorter Alpine hiking loop? Or maybe we'd just find a nice place and stay there.

We wanted to keep our options open. What difference would it really make anyway?

2. Countdown

It wasn't quite the smell of freedom and the great outdoors that greeted us as we stepped out of Geneva airport on that first, humid evening. It was the smell of exhaust fumes. It was 9 p.m. and as thousands of business commuters, holiday makers and airport employees vanished into the Geneva suburbs, we took our first fully laden steps. We had 5 kilometres of cycle tracks and pavements to tackle, as well as a national border to cross, before we reached our budget hotel room.

The sky was dark by the time we reached the Hotel F1 in France, just a few hundred metres beyond an unlit and unmanned customs post straddling a deserted country lane. Our route had taken us passed the swanky, expensive hotels close to the airport before meandering through a series of nondescript Swiss backwaters and then, finally, rural France. In all that time we'd never been more than a hundred metres from the airport perimeter fence, watching the final few flights of the day gliding in to land.

This was the first time we'd stayed with this European one-star hotel chain, so didn't know what to expect for our thirty euros. First impressions were a little off-putting, with a silent orchestra of chain smoking, eastern European truck drivers creating a tunnel of smoke and staring at us as we entered the tiny reception. A few minutes later we had checked in but still felt somewhat intimidated. The setting of the sun had introduced a welcome coolness to the air outside, but it was yet to penetrate the oppressive, narrow corridors. Setting off in search of our room we passed open door after open door, revealing more groups of young men lounging on bunk beds, playing cards and staring as we passed. It was a relief when we closed our own door behind us.

The room itself was designed for sleeping and nothing else. Showers and toilets were communal, so other than a sink and two single beds bolted to the floor we had no creature comforts, which of course was all we needed. We were, after all, planning to be sleeping in a tent fairly soon and had not been expecting a luxury suite. What was less comfortable was the sauna like temperature radiating from every surface. With a single, closed, west-facing window, the hot afternoon sun had enjoyed plenty of time to bring the walls and furniture up to a gentle simmer. We cracked the window open the permitted maximum of two inches, parked our bags, rinsed our single set of sweaty clothes in the sink and lay naked and unmoving on the bunks trying not to evaporate. We could hear the loitering crowds shuffling about outside, so propping our door open did not seem an option, especially with my stewed plums on display. We didn't feel unsafe, just slightly claustrophobic.

Sleep finally arrived and it turned out to be a very quiet night. Truck drivers trapped in hot hotel rooms in rural France, it seems, are not looking for a party. By the time we had reloaded our packs and set off the next morning, to walk back into Geneva centre, most of the drivers and trucks had already vanished.

We had visited Geneva once before, during our first summer as a couple fifteen years earlier. Back then we'd been students travelling on an Interrail ticket. While many of our friends had sought out CV boosting internships, we had each applied for, and secured, a travel bursary from college. Armed with ludicrously bulky rucksacks, a tent, lilos in the shape of a lighthouse to sleep on and an eyesore of a bumbag strapped around our waist for 'valuables', most of which consisted of dozens of rolls of spent camera film, we set off on our first ever adventure together. For the princely sum of £180 we had bought a train ticket valid on almost every single train across eight countries for an entire month and we certainly put it to good use, taking upwards of sixty individual journeys totalling more than 2500 miles! We visited Salzburg, Vienna, Venice, Geneva, Lausanne, Zurich, Copenhagen and dozens of other places in between.

Geneva, in fact, had featured in one of our more memorable train experiences. We'd caught a night train out of Venice at around 10 p.m., primarily in order to avoid forking out for another expensive hotel room. We'd only been in Italy for a few days and were already sick of the place. The pushing, the noise, the heat, the traffic, the shouting, the apparent lack of campsites...I accept that Venice is hardly representative of the whole country but two days of shuffling, armpit to armpit, with the summer hordes alongside mosquito heaving canals had driven us to seek out somewhere less manic. Where better, we reasoned, than the land of bank clerks, tax avoidance and Julie Andrews singing in the mountains.

For approximately 8 hours we'd rattled slowly through the night in an oppressively hot 6-seater train compartment, while creepy characters in the teeming corridor had taken turns to stare at us and our luggage. Sleep had been elusive, partly because we were forced to remain bolt upright along with the other four occupants of our sweaty booth but also as a result of the frequent, back-jarring emergency stops the train driver saw fit to inflict on us all. It was around 3 a.m. and following one especially violent halt, that my rucksack decided it had also had enough and so made a bid for freedom. One moment I was looking across at a rather prim, petite lady trying her best to nod off, the next a 4-foot tower of green fabric and padded straps with twitching legs sticking out from underneath it. "Oh, Mama Mia" she exclaimed (yes, people really say that). I was just glad she was still alive. My rucksack weighed about 25 kg on that trip and had only just missed the top of her head. It was an incident that didn't help to improve the mood in the carriage. Then, to top it all off, we rolled into Genoa! Talk about a balls up. It took us another 6 hours to finally get to Geneva after doubling back to Milan. We still had a lovely time in Geneva though. Despite the city feeling rather bland and without character in itself there had at least been a funfair taking place on the shores of Lac Leman. In fact, during the clearing out that preceded the adventure in this book, I came across a promotional condom that had been thrust into my hand alongside the dodgems (OK, so perhaps that's a bad choice of words). It worked though, the advertising I mean. If I ever spend time in Geneva I'll definitely be listening to "One FM 107, La Radio Hit".

This second visit to Switzerland's second most populous city was much more practical and brief. We found the bus station, got on a bus and left Switzerland completely. Our destination for the day was the lakeside town of Thonon-les-Bains, just across the border in France and one of two possible starting points for the Alpine section of the GR5 outlined in our guidebook, "The GR5 Trail" by Paddy Dillon (Cicerone Guides). I must admit, I hadn't actually read this guidebook in any detail at this point. I'd tried a couple of times, usually while sat on the toilet, but on each occasion had quickly zoned out and gotten lost among the detailed twists and turns. Although I'm an avid reader, every time I read a travel book and see the name of a place I haven't visited, except perhaps major cities, I just don't take it in. The writing can be beautiful and I can be fully immersed in the book, but when it comes to unfamiliar place names all my brain registers is "mnhhh".

As Esther had learned to her cost over the years, I have a great memory for numbers, such as the frequency of the radio station advertised on my souvenir condom, but wordy details like shopping lists and directions just don't stick. I have occasionally tried to make a special effort to notice place names in books, but all that proved was that unless a place has a funny name, like "Plop" or "Fanny", I'll forget it by the next day anyway. Therefore, although I'd agreed to be responsible for checking the route ahead, I'd not done much beyond having a cursory scan of the opening few days and double-checking the place we needed to start.

Besides, it had been so long since we'd actually done any hiking with full packs on our backs that the numerical details of the hike were far too abstract to mean anything. Timings, distances and altitudes, which the guide contained in abundance, did not automatically conjure up an image of how a day would actually 'feel'. I knew it would be hard and physically demanding but I also assumed we'd be up to the task when the time came, regardless of what the numbers were. We'd always been sporty and had remained pretty active during our two years of motorhome touring, with plenty of day hikes and long bike rides. Our weight and fitness had varied with the seasons, leaner in summer, a little heavier in winter, but we'd never been really unfit. We'd even had a temporary gym membership during our first couple of months back in the UK which we'd made good use of. Granted, any good work in the gym had almost certainly been erased during our final two months in the UK, which had involved much more dairy-free ice cream and late nights dealing with 'stuff' than exercise, but in a perverse way that just made me more excited. It wasn't just the Alps I was going to conquer, it was also going to be goodbye love handles and hello six-pack. I was pretty sure Esther felt similarly, or at least I hoped so, because the truth is that we hadn't talked about the physical effort side of things. The small amount of conversation we did have about the route ahead tended to focus on how we could always change our minds and do something else if it wasn't working out.

Maybe it was because of this lack of commitment, but on the bus to Thonon-les-Bains we decided not to hit the trail immediately. Instead we elected to take a couple of extra days 'resting' before we headed into the wilderness, booking into a cheap(ish) hotel room near Thonon-les-Bains bus station for two nights. Once settled we set about doing various things completely unrelated to hiking. There was some last-minute administration related to our Egypt trip in a month's time to start with, plus a lie-in to enjoy and a couple of picnics on the shores of Lac Leman. We even found time to slip on the trainers we'd packed and go jogging, twice. In fact, as we slowly meandered around Thonon-les-Bains wearing the few 'normal clothes' we'd packed, it was hard to believe we were about to venture out of civilisation at all. Although we'd never actually taken a city break in the past, this was a lot like I imagined one would be. We couldn't even see any mountains behind the passing clouds.

The only slight nod we made towards our imminent hike was popping into a local bookshop to try and buy a map of the opening part of the route, which we failed to do, but we did come away with an excellent French guidebook instead. Just like our Cicerone guide, the "Grande Traversée des Alpes - Du Léman à la Vanoise" by TopoGuides described (in French) the route of the GR5 from Lac Leman as far as Landry, about ten days of hiking away, but more importantly contained the relevant sections of Ordnance Survey style maps and brilliant altitude profiles. With Paddy's English language description from the "The GR5 Trail" alongside the maps in this French guide book, we felt much more reassured that we'd make it safely through the opening six days of hiking we expected it would take us to reach Chamonix. That was the number of days that Paddy broke this opening part of the route, which he called "Stage 1", into. Apparently, it was also possible to complete stage 1 even faster, in just five days, by starting at a place called St Gingolph a bit further along the shores of Lac Leman, but Thonon-les-Bains had been both easier and cheaper for us to reach from Geneva. Plus, the opening two days from Thonon-les-Bains were described by Paddy as "longer, but easier". Starting off gently sounded good.

Still, by the time we put our heads down for our second and final night in Thonon-les-Bains there were a few butterflies in our tummies. It had been fun to put our heads in the sand and potter around Thonon-les-Bains for two days but, short of booking another night and hiding in our room the following day, in just a few hours' time we would be heading off into an unfamiliar wilderness. Ahead of us

14

were hundreds of remote kilometres and tens of thousands of metres of climbing to haul our unconditioned bodies across. It should have been exciting. It was what we had flown across Europe to do, probably, yet the closer we came to departure the less and less of a good idea it felt. In our haste to do something, anything, to quickly resolve the 'living-out-of-boxes' situation we'd steered ourselves into, and in our excitement to finally have a crack at the GR5, it was dawning on us that perhaps we hadn't quite given this adventure the respect it deserved.

3. Reluctantly Into The Wild

General wisdom dictates that if you're going to go walking in the mountains then you should set off as early in the morning as possible. It's not masochism, as applicable as that word might seem when describing people who choose to walk up steep hills for hours on end. There is, in fact, a genuinely very good reason for early starts. On a meteorological scale, mountains are much more than lumpy bits of earth that are nice to look at, they are also weather making factories. You can wake up to clear skies, coat yourself with sun cream against the raging UV and sweat uphill until your clothes are sodden and then, just as you're sitting down to lunch miles from shelter, the clouds will start to gather. One minute the air can be the essence of tranquillity and the next minute you can have icy daggers trying to pierce your eyelids. The trouble is, like Forrest Gump's 'box of chocolates', you never quite know what you're going to get. Sometimes storms start at midday, sometimes it rains in the evening, sometimes clouds don't appear at all. In the mountains it can downpour for a week, or it can stay dry for a month. The power of forecasts only goes so far and, as a result, the only real insurance policy for avoiding a soaking and unnecessary danger in the wilderness is to get your boots on and get cracking with the dawn.

Still, you don't always have to listen to common sense. Do you? Instead of being suited and booted with the dawn, racing to put our feet on the trail at first light on this first day of our four-week hiking odyssey, we opted to have a lie-in instead. Having essentially raced to Switzerland on a whim, and without any real commitment to a clear goal or concrete plan for the next four weeks, we decided to adventurously suck every last drop of warmth and safety from our hotel room before giving up the key. I even had

16

two showers, for no better reason than because I could and because I was reluctant to say farewell to on-tap hot water.

Then, naturally, we had to do some last-minute re-organising of our gear as well. We could have done this the night before, but we hadn't. Even if it was too late to actually shave off any weight we at least wanted to make our packs look a respectable shape. Our initial round of packing had taken place on my in-laws living room floor the night before we'd left the UK. This had involved emptying the two boxes containing our assortment of 'hiking and outdoor gear' onto the carpet and then spending half an hour on our hands and knees jamming things into our packs. The result, visually at least, was that it looked like we were smuggling a family of oversized garden gnomes.

There were three basic categories of stuff we'd bought with us. Things we (a) definitely needed, (b) wanted and (c) couldn't make our minds up about. At Heathrow airport my lumpy 58 litre pack had weighed in at a whopping 18 kg, while Esther's top heavy 46 litre pack had tipped the scales at 13 kg. This did not include the extra bits and bobs we had in carrier bags because we hadn't been able to get them into our rucksacks. Now, 31 kg between two people (before water) is, to be blunt, a bastard heavy weight to carry over mountain passes for a month.

It wasn't that we had too much 'crap' hiking gear with us. A few years earlier that would have been the case, but not anymore. Gone was the 2 kg 'portable' CD player that we had hauled with us on our Interrail travels. Gone were the sleeping bags which packed away to the size, and weight, of beer kegs. We'd even, finally, gotten rid of Esther's prized first set of trekking poles which once prompted a fellow hiker, who had picked them up, to ask "what do you use these for, bludgeoning cows to death?" No, this time the reason for our overladen packs wasn't down to an abundance of heavy fleeces, sweat-inducing rubber waterproofs or even unnecessary electronics. Instead we'd just gotten trapped by indecision. Put simply, because we were trying to keep our options open, we hadn't been entirely sure what sort of adventure we were packing for.

Our essential hiking equipment, the bits that fell into the (a) category, was mostly made up of expensive, lightweight, branded stuff chosen especially because it didn't weigh very much. It's not like we were complete hiking novices and had, in recent years at least, invested in some pretty decent kit. We're talking carbon fibre trekking poles, titanium saucepan and sporks, down jackets and sleeping bags, featherlight air mattresses, the works. Even the rucksacks we had were from an ultralight product line saving an extra kilogram at least on conventional packs.

The problem we had was that filling the gaps surrounding all this expensive gear was a bunch of other stuff of questionable use. With 'backpacking' on buses and trains still a possible part of this adventure, or maybe even staying in one place for an extended period of time, we'd also packed things like 'smart' clothes for wearing around town, a yoga belt for stretching at the end of the day, a reusable shopping bag for visiting supermarkets, trainers to go jogging, two glass jars of a green supplement powder because we were worried about eating enough fresh veggies, and a bunch of other 'spares' just in case. We had three ways of sterilising water, two ways of heating it up and our first aid kit wouldn't have looked out of place in a battle zone, with dressings of all sizes, creams and lotions for stings, burns, cuts and grazes, pills for most eventualities and implements to remove a bullet (well, splinters and ticks anyway). Then, to top it all off, because we were worried about finding high calorie, plant-based food on the trail that wasn't solely dry bread and pasta, we were hauling about 5 kg of backup food that we'd picked up in the UK.

Obviously packing and pack weight is a personal thing, but I think that Paddy Dillon puts it rather well in the "The GR5 Trail" when he says "carrying a heavy pack is

18

hard work but tents and sleeping bags can be lightweight and strong, so pack weight need not be excessive and certainly not more than 10kg (22lb), with tent, before adding food and water. It will seldom be necessary to pack more than a day's worth of food, and water is available at regular intervals". Wow, it sounds so sensible when he writes it like that. If only I'd read that before we set out from Thonon-les-Bains.

What I did know at the time, however, was that there is a class of ultralight hikers who claim to be able to get their pack weight down to just 5 or 6 kg, including full camping gear, by sleeping on the earth under a tarpaulin, making their own methylated spirit burners out of cat food tins and snapping their toothbrush in half.

In these final minutes before we joined the GR5 it was fairly obvious to us that we'd made a bit of a packing error. Gravity is a relentless companion, it doesn't take breaks. At a time when every extra gram counted, we'd gone and packed for more than one type of trip. Unfortunately, short of giving up before taking a single step, there wasn't a lot we could do about it now, except perhaps snapping our toothbrushes in half, which we did. Actually, we went a step further because, since we know each other quite well, we decided to share half a toothbrush. Some people may find this off-putting, but there's nothing that says "I love you" more than passing your partner the crusty nub of a brush and saying "go on, you go first".

So it was that, after discarding about 1.5 grams of plastic toothbrush handle, we shouldered our burdens, pulled our hip straps as tight as possible to spread the load, and prepared to set off. At first it didn't even feel that heavy and I felt quite impressed with myself. "Ooh, look how strong I am" I thought. I admit I even managed to derive an extra bit of satisfaction out of having such a stupidly heavy pack. It would only make what we were about to do even more of an achievement. Wouldn't it?

There was, however, one arguably unnecessary passenger who we were definitely glad to have on board, deadweight or not. Gerald the Giraffe had been on pretty much every trip we'd ever taken since we'd found him in a Viennese toy shop on our first Interrail adventure. Standing at a towering 3 inches high and tipping the scales at eye-watering 25 grams, we wanted to make sure our fluffy little pal had a front row seat to whatever lay ahead. Perched on my right shoulder, with his rear end nestled in the little pouch designed to hold the end of my drinking tube and his 'safety harness' (keyring chain) securely fastened around a strap I never found another use for, he certainly looked the most comfortable of our group as we took our first steps south out of Thonon-les-Bains.

As with most major trails in the French Alps, GR5 waymarkers consist of a white and red dash, one above the other. Within a few minutes of leaving our hotel we had found our first of the adventure next to Thonon-les-Bains train station. Even though we'd only been officially on the trail for a matter of seconds, we still took a moment to pause and reflect on the amazing fact that this was just one in an (almost) unbroken chain of markers running for 2300 km, appearing on signposts, trees and boulders all the way from the North Sea to the Mediterranean!

By now it was early afternoon and as we crossed the railway bridge an alarming burn appeared almost immediately in my thighs and I found myself sweating already in the oppressively hot and muggy air, perfect weather for afternoon storms. "Oi, stop it" I thought as I willed my body not to feel pain so easily, "you're fitter than this, I know you are and we have a long way to go".

Having undertaken no in-depth planning of our own and with no accommodation booked along the hundreds of kilometres of trail ahead, our intention was to basically stick to the stages suggested in "The GR5 Trail" and find places to camp as and when required. In practice, on this first day, that meant we had about 8 hours left before dark to reach the village of Chevenoz, a mere 25 km and a suggested 7 hours of walking time away, with 1090 metres of ascent and 545 metres of descent added in for good measure. Surely our fit, well-rested bodies could manage that.

Following the red and white markers we soon left buildings and tarmac behind us and found ourselves on dirt tracks that climbed gently, but constantly, alongside open pastures and through wooded areas. Occasional glimpses of distant rocky peaks through the mist and clouds helped to give a small sense of progress and overcome some of the unspoken doubts that had crept in during our sluggish start to the day. Despite dragging our feet at the prospect of leaving urban comforts behind, it felt good to be on the trail and back out in the wild, free, open air. Other than our trekking poles clicking out a steady rhythm on the ground and the sound of the breeze stirring the long grass, there wasn't a lot of background noise to disturb the natural beauty around us. Life, in those opening moments, felt very good.

Probably because of this good feeling combined with adrenalin, and probably also because neither of us wanted the other to see us struggling, for the first hour or so we both managed to stay proudly upright beneath our heavy packs. But we couldn't pretend forever. Our ultralight packs were by far the most comfortable we'd ever owned, they fitted our contours magnificently, but it wasn't long before the incessant tug of gravity began pulling our shoulders forward and we gradually began to lean into our packs like Arctic explorers man-hauling heavy sleds. "Just keep walking" we'd smile to each other as we marched along at a firm pace, sweat rolling off our brows and soaking through the clothes on our backs and thighs. "Just keep walking". It became a bit of a mantra.

We managed almost two hours before our first, brief pause and a further two hours after that before our next, slightly longer rest. By now it was early evening and, with at least three more hours of hiking predicted by the guidebook, it was becoming clear that we wouldn't make it to Chevenoz before dark after all, not if we wanted the freedom to take any more breaks and have some dinner anyway. I suppose I'd been hoping that some sort of innate hiking ability we possessed would see us forging ahead of the 7 hours suggested hiking time, but if anything we were lagging behind.

It was a dent to my confidence and a challenge to my ego that was for sure. As a result, in the first of many similar gripes to come in the week ahead, I found myself questioning what sort of nuclear driven cyborg had power marched at warp speed in order to arrive at the timings suggested in the "bastard guidebook" anyway. The directions were all well and good, but no matter how fast we moved our feet we were consistently 20-30% slower to each village or marker. "Damn you Paddy Dillon" I found myself cursing. "This book is supposed to be written with your average hiker carrying camping gear in mind" I loudly complained, "not some super-walker flouncing along with just a hanky and a sodding credit card in their pocket. Paddy Dillon. Paddy effing Power more like. Bastard! No, no, Double Bastard!" Esther, for her part, agreed that the suggested timings seemed a little ambitious, but used far fewer swear words than I did.

Moving slower than the guidebook was hardly a logistical disaster. We could always pitch our tent in a field once the sun began to set and just set off early the next morning. We'd done it in the past and knew that bivouacking, the French term for pitching a small tent for a single night and moving on with no trace, was usually legal in France provided it was done discretely and the site chosen met certain criteria. But it was still humbling and a little disappointing.

We cooked our dinner in the village of Reyvroz at 776 metres altitude, having ascended around 400 metres during our first 13 kilometres of walking. Sharing a pack of edamame bean pasta followed by some oats, almond butter and dried fruit mix prepared from the supplies we'd bought from the UK was divine. After the sweating and the alarmingly swift onset of aching backs and sore shoulders, it was a welcome reminder of the heightened pleasures long distance hiking can provide to balance the discomforts. In a life where the floor serves as a combined chair, table and bed and where rivers and streams act as both showers and water sources, every meal can feel like a banquet and every picnic bench a throne.

It was still early evening when we set off again, but almost immediately I had a problem. I needed a toilet, urgently. I've been bowel incontinent my entire life due to a birth defect called imperforate anus. I was born with a serious deformation in the plumbing around my rear end and underwent a series of surgeries as a new-born, first to save my life and then to create the missing parts. As a result, everything has always looked cosmetically normal on the outside but, unfortunately, my man-made plumbing has never worked as it was supposed to. I went on to spend the best part of my first thirty years on Earth hiding and downplaying the frequency and severity of the accidents I was having, dozens of them every day, to everyone including my parents and doctors before finally asking for help.

It is a subject about which I could write an entire book so I'm not going to go into it too much here, except to say that when I need to go, I really need to go, because I can't hold it in. Also, in a somewhat cruel irony, I can't actually push it out either. Instead, once I become aware of the need to go, I have to use an enema kit which flushes me out for anything between 12-24 hours. At home, in daily life, this is usually straightforward but on a hiking expedition it is less easy. Ducking behind a big tree or crouching in some long grass for a few minutes, for instance, isn't really an option for me. I have used my enema kit in the great outdoors on overnight hiking trips in the past, usually heating up the water on our burner after dark, digging a hole and then squatting in a hidden place for the thirty or forty minutes it usually takes to evacuate (that's the technical term by the way, I don't mean run off). Unfortunately, dropping my trousers and standing around for half an hour with a plastic pipe stuck up my backside is usually frowned upon in urban environments and so the centre of Reyvroz wasn't going to get to see that show. I certainly wouldn't have known the French to explain what I was doing. ("Bonjour Monsieur Gendarme. Non, non, je ne suis pas un pervert").

After wasting half an hour waddling up and down the deserted streets of Reyvroz it was clear that the few signposted 'toilettes' were either already locked for the night or had been boarded up in disrepair and it drove me to take drastic action. For many years beforehand I would have simply refused to ask for help. Despite only having a single pair of trousers with me and only one spare pair of underpants, I still probably would have struggled onwards into the wilderness, getting into a progressively worse mess as I went. I would have continued to clean myself up as best as I could, whenever the opportunity arose, and for however long it took until either I found a toilet or came across a spot so secluded and quiet I would have risked using my enema kit outdoors in daylight.

Yet on this occasion, on this first day of our adventure, I did something I had never done before. I asked for the help of a stranger. Esther, with great foresight, had written out a card for me in various languages explaining my condition and asking if I could use a toilet and some warm water. It was a somewhat momentous, not to mention frightening, step for me when I knocked on a stranger's door for the first time and showed them what I hoped was a correctly translated and polite request. "Hello, can you please help me. I am on a hiking trip but I have a medical condition. Bowel incontinence. I need to use a toilet and cannot find one nearby. Would it be possible for me to use

24

your toilet for half an hour? I also need a litre of warm water if possible. Thank you."

An hour later I was thanking the elderly couple who had extended their hospitality and opened their home to me. Not only had they allowed a particularly dishevelled looking, sweaty and smelly stranger to cross their threshold based only on a few scribbled sentences, they had also given me the space and privacy to do what I needed to do without asking any questions. Words can't express how much relief I had felt the moment they had read my card and said "oui, bien sûr".

Another hour of much more comfortable walking later, following a gradual descent on muddy paths through more fields, we reached the hamlet of Bioge and were definitely ready to stop for the night. The sky was darkening and the clouds building fast. Spotting an outdoor activities centre by the trail we noticed the staff preparing to leave for the night, packing away an array wetsuits and rafts. Wandering over, Esther explained in her best French that we were walking the GR5 and needed a place to camp. Would they mind, she asked, if we camped on their field? We promised to be gone by 7 a.m.

At first it looked doubtful. Normally, they explained, they could not allow any camping and if they'd had customers arriving early the next morning they would have had to say no. However, it just so happened they had no groups until the following afternoon and so, on this one rare occasion, it was OK. We were so relieved. Not only did this mean we had found a place to camp and had acquired the owner's permission, but there were even outdoor toilet facilities that we could use. Double bonus! But the best was yet to come. Pointing to a cluster of giant teepees erected on the field we were planning to camp on they said "choose one, you can sleep in those". We didn't even have to put up our own tent! We offered money, but they wouldn't accept anything.

Collapsing onto our air mattresses in the spacious expanse of our own wooden-floored private teepee for the night, I felt incredibly relieved to be undercover and that our adventure was properly underway. We'd survived our first day and hiked for more than five hours, I'd been able to access toilets when required and we'd ended up sleeping in far more comfort than I'd ever expected. My confidence, which had been more up and down than the trail so far, was going to bed on a high. We were even going to bed clean, having secretly stripped off after the staff left to give each other an icy hosing down with the pipe usually reserved for cleaning wetsuits. Not quite a warm shower but much better than going to bed still wearing the greasy mix of sun-cream and insect repellent we'd accumulated during the afternoon. Things seemed to be working out after all.

We may only have walked for five hours and completed two thirds of the guidebook version of 'Day 1', but I reasoned that our bodies were still getting used to the trail and our packs were especially heavily laden with the food from the UK. Hoping for a good night's sleep and basking in the warm glow of the kindness of strangers, it didn't take long before I slipped into surprisingly comfortable oblivion.

Vital Statistics - Day 1
Start: Thonon-les-Bains
End: Bioge
Distance Hiked: 17 kilometres
Hiking Time: 5 hours
Height Gain: 600 metres
Height Loss: 400 metres

4. The Only Way Is Up, Apparently

Relief and pain. Emotion and sensation. These were the first two things I noticed as the unwelcome honking of our alarm stirred me into consciousness. Relief because the overnight storms that had battered the teepee had vanished. Pain because my back, hips, neck and buttocks had seized the opportunity, while I slept, to grow bruises. "Welcome to day two you mug" they seemed to be saying to me.

Stepping out of the teepee into a misty morning, we breathed in fresh, moist air heavy with the smell of the fir trees decorating the valley sides all around us. "Much better than caffeine" I thought, which was good since we didn't have any tea or coffee with us. It was just after 7 a.m. and since we had fallen behind our guidebook dictated 'schedule' the previous afternoon, our aim was to use this much earlier start to try and get back on terms with Mr Paddy Power by the end of the day. First, we had to reach the village of Chevenoz to complete 'Day 1', only 8 km and 500 odd metres of climbing away, and then tackle 'Day 2', which promised an additional 22 km of hiking with 1730 metres of ascent and 1625 metres of descent. The total time for this combined undertaking was suggested by Paddy to be around 11 hours. Well, we had all day and I genuinely felt it would be much easier than the day before somehow, now that we'd started to find our feet and all.

The trail was uphill from the moment we set off out of Bioge, climbing mostly gradually but with some especially steep sections on winding, forested paths that were muddy and slippery after the overnight storms. About twenty minutes after setting off a momentary break in the mist and cloud coincided with a break in the trees revealing, for just a few seconds, a stunning glance of the distant summit of Mont Blanc. A teaser of the route ahead. I've always found it an odd sensation, on a long hike, to look at a distant location that could be reached in a matter of minutes using modern transport and reflect on just how long it will take to reach on foot. When I'm feeling negative the effect is to further enhance my low mood, reminding me that the effort and discomfort of the hike had been optional. When I'm feeling good, however, it just makes me excited at what adventures are still to come. Such was the case on this second day of our long walk south. Good times lay ahead I felt.

The muddy tracks soon gave way to sections of tarmac passing through various small hamlets, still climbing with every step. After a couple of hours we officially finished Paddy's 'Day 1'. We celebrated on the outskirts of Chevenoz by taking our first brief pause of the day, unshouldering our packs and leaning our sweaty backs, glamorously, against a rusty roadside crash barrier. We'd climbed a shade over 500 metres already, with a net gain of about 400 metres so far. Fortunately, the low morning mist had also gone uphill at a similar rate to us and so it still hung just over our heads rather than surrounding us completely. It was a trend that would, thankfully, continue throughout the day.

After nibbling a few almonds and raisins, the next portion of the trail saw us leaving the tarmac and hamlets behind. All being well it would be only grass, mud and rock for at least the next 22 km until the village of La Chappelle d'Abondance and the end of 'Day 2'. The next hour and a half consisted of more gently sloping fields and steeply climbing forest tracks, where tall pines vanished upwards into the mist creating a mystical ambiance, until we came upon a collection of cowsheds identified by Paddy as Le Grand Chesnay. "Perfect", we thought. Not only was this clearly a good place for cows to spend their winters, but with a water source that the nearby herd seemed happy to share and having already climbed another 450 metres since Chevenoz, we decided it was an ideal place to take an early lunch ourselves. Never before have buckwheat Ramen noodles with miso seasoning, yet more of UK supplies, tasted so good. What we didn't know was that this would be the last really relaxed moment of the day.

We tried to get going again after food but evidently our energetic morning, and the relatively fast pace we'd been setting, with over 1000 metres of climbing and almost 900 metres net gain in the past three and half hours, had taken more out of us than we'd realised. Full tummies didn't help either. We were definitely feeling far less sprightly with a bellyful of noodles sloshing about inside of us, but still the path just continued to go up and up, just like it had all morning, except that now it was doing so frustratingly slowly. Steep enough to drain our energy but not steep enough to feel like we were getting anywhere. Various named places and route markers noted by Paddy came and went, yet the scenery didn't seem to be changing. The views were pleasant enough, with plenty of rolling hills, trees and far reaching panoramas over Lac Leman, which was now almost a vertical mile below us, but frankly it would have been easier if it had been steeper and rockier so that the 'progress' we were making could have been more noticeable. After a while the scenery almost began to blur into a monotonous green-brown smudge with a lake in the background as we continued our relentless plod. We weren't supposed to be feeling like this on just our second day, surely?

By the time we reached the open crest of Tête des Fieux at 1772 metres, with a total hiking time approaching 7 hours for the day, we were physically and emotionally done in and ready to stop. Perhaps even to call the whole adventure off. The view was great, but in our grouchy states we were barely able to appreciate it. Our stops over the previous three and a half hours, since our noodley lunch, had become increasingly frequent. At first, feeling the tiredness setting in, we'd tried to use sugary snacks to help us keep going and maintain the pace we needed to set to complete 'Day 2', but had then run out of dried fruit and nut snacks as well. Now, not only were we knackered and feeling a massive dip in blood sugar, but the only food we had left needed cooking and we couldn't be bothered to get the necessary kit out.

Esther was especially struggling and I hadn't done much to help on that front recently. A short while earlier we had been passed by our first 'Speedy Gonzalez', a young man with a GR5 guidebook strapped to the outside of his pack who flew past us with scarcely a bead of sweat on his brow nor a grunt of acknowledgement, which had left me feeling somewhat challenged and inadequate. When he'd paused to eat a pack of biscuits a little way ahead of us, I'd found myself puffing out my chest like an insecure pigeon and power marching to get ahead of him again, which had the unfortunate side effect of leaving Esther far behind. After about thirty minutes of letting him know that "I could go faster if I wanted to, I just don't feel like it right now, OK mister", I then had to stop and let him pass me a second time while Esther caught up (and I got my breath back). To be honest I wasn't entirely sure whether I'd been trying to prove something to myself or Speedy? Maybe both? Either way, as exhaustion had heightened both of our subsequent emotions, the upshot was that Esther felt she couldn't keep up and was holding me back while I felt guilty for being an egoic tit. Our uncertain and fluctuating mood took another dip. Perhaps we had bitten off more than we could chew after all? Was this adventure really such a good idea?

As late afternoon began to turn into early evening, and the clouds began to darken threateningly again, we couldn't avoid the fact that as much as we wanted to stop it simply wasn't an option right now. There were few places nearby flat enough to set up a tent and we had very little water left. According to Paddy there was, a short distance ahead, a small lake called Lac de la Case at 1750 metres where we guessed we might camp before the darkening clouds began to produce rain. We could just about see it, beautifully nestled beneath the towering crags of Dent d'Oche high above. That was one option, but the downside would be that when we woke up the next day we'd still have another eight or nine hundred metres of ascending and almost a mile of descending, which Paddy estimated at over 5 hours of hiking, to reach La Chapelle d'Abondance and complete 'Day 2'. That would be punishing enough in itself and we'd never be able to make a start on 'Day 3'. On the other hand, if we could somehow find the energy to push on and were willing to risk being rained on over the highpoint of the day, the Col de Pavis at 1944 metres, we could perhaps make it to the place called Chalets de Bise (1506 metres) and be within just a couple of hours of finishing 'Day 2'.

Our sugar starved brains weren't exactly in prime decision-making form, which maybe explains why we decided to keep walking and "push on" over the Col de Pavis. Or maybe it was still too deeply ingrained in our 'high-flier' life conditioning to attack adversity rather than accept a change of plan at this point, even if it would have been a more sensible choice. Either way, spurred on by the adrenalin of racing the impending bad weather combined with the thrill of entering into the rocky, boulder strewn cauldron leading up to the col, with sheer cliff faces towering over us as we approached 2000 metres altitude, we accelerated. After a day and a half of hiking through fields and trees the climb to the Col de Pavis made us feel properly back in the mountains. It was visually stunning, still surrounded by a sea of green but almost as though the rolling fields had sprouted teeth of rock. We even had our own furry fan club, with several goggle-eyed chamois staring open mouthed at us from their invisible perches on the apparently smooth cliffs above us. After feeling so shattered just minutes before it was as though we had come to life again. Our bodies were digging deep to take us where we had decided to go. It was the first time we'd moved faster than Paddy, proof positive that it could be done, even by wallies like us hauling too much gear.

It was just before dark when we reached Chalets de Bise, a small cluster of buildings offering food but no public toilet facilities, which was a little disappointing. Thankfully, for me, I didn't yet need any. Instead we hastily joined the small cluster of tents pitched by the side of the narrow access road and within less than half an hour, just as the rain finally arrived, we were sliding into our sleeping bags for our first night under canvas.

In total we had hiked for almost nine hours, chalking up around 1900 metres of ascent, 900 metres of descent and covered close to 25 km of trail since we had left Bioge. If someone had told me after lunch, when I'd been tightening my hipstraps beneath a belly bursting with Ramen noodles, that we would go on to hike for another five and a half hours and climb another 1000 metres that same day, I would not have believed it. Yet we had done so. Mentally I chalked it up as a big achievement.

Even better, despite the many moments of tension and extreme fatigue, we hadn't had an argument! Not even so much as cross word. So many times, in our shared past, things like doubts over route choices combined with physical exhaustion would have seen us bickering at the very least and more likely outright shouting. After almost fifteen years together we knew exactly which buttons to press to let the other know we were pissed off, but then pretend we weren't. "Well, isn't this a great idea of '*ours*'. I'm having such a 'great' time."......"What do you mean, this was your idea to start with"......"No, it bloody wasn't. And why are you being so moody anyway, I only said I was having a good time"......"No, you didn't. You said '*great*' time, I know what you meant. And, by the way, why do you always get to go first with the toothbrush......" And so it might have continued.

But it hadn't happened. I hadn't tried to be Mr Fix It and downplay Esther's struggle, while Esther had encouraged me and reassured me that she'd tell me if she needed my help. There had been no blame either way, just a mutual determination and compassion.

Like greasy, sweaty, monster caterpillars in our lime green sleeping bags, we romantically tilted our tired torsos a few inches towards each other and kissed each other goodnight. I'd been nervous about adapting to tent-bound sleeping, but I was so tired that unconsciousness arrived just a few minutes later.

Vital Statistics - Day 2
Start: Bioge
End: Chalets de Bise
Distance Hiked: 25 kilometres
Hiking Time: 9 hours
Height Gain: 1900 metres
Height Loss: 900 metres

5. Get A Room

I suppose, in hindsight, the argument we ended up having shortly after finally setting off on our third day of hiking was one of the best things that could have happened.

The rather urgent need to give myself an enema had driven me out of my sleeping bag a little before 5 a.m. I'd love to say it woke me, but sadly I was already awake. I was also soggy. Another overnight deluge had highlighted the fact that we'd inadvertently pitched our little tent in an otherwise invisible dip in the ground. Sometime in the early hours our tent had become an island state. Our groundsheet had done a great job of holding back several inches of standing water, but there was little it could do to stop the water being splashed up and under the tarpaulin and onto our inner tent, from where it had trickled silently beneath our sleeping bodies. By the time we realised we were sleeping in a puddle there wasn't much we could do about it, except pile our possessions on top of aching bodies, tuck up tightly in the foetal position and try and sleep a little while longer. Still, at least the rain had stopped by the time I needed an enema.

Heating up a litre of water in the slowly gathering light of dawn, before wandering off to find a quiet, out of sight spot to do what I needed to do was a bit of double-edged sword. On the one hand the damp mountain air smelled amazing and the peacefulness of watching the sun creep down the steep sides of the valley we were camping in was a moment to treasure. I had the wilderness entirely to myself, alone in the Alps. I could have been the only human alive in that moment and it was blissful. On the other hand, having to half-squat over a rock, naked from the waist down for half an hour with mosquitoes swarming around my bare buttocks somewhat blunted the tranquillity.

Back at our island paradise by 6 a.m. I decided there was no point going back to bed. I was up and dressed and

34

definitely fully awake. I figured that as soon as Esther was ready we might as well be off. Hopefully we could get another early start and make up a little time. It turned out to be a surprisingly long wait.

As nearby campers began to emerge from their tents, bleary-eyed and spending far longer brewing up coffee than it took to pack away their gear, Esther stayed firmly in her sleeping bag. 7 a.m. came and went, then 8 a.m., and still I stood alone. Exhausted is one word for how Esther was feeling, but broken would perhaps be more accurate. Just three years earlier Esther had been seriously unwell. Apart from forcing herself out of the house to meet personal training clients, all her body could manage between sessions was to collapse and sleep. Some days, when we tried to go for a walk to unwind, she'd not been able to walk more than a few hundred metres from the car. She was functioning pretty much on willpower alone and we'd been terrified about what the cause might be. Several months and numerous hospital visits and tests later, Esther had been diagnosed with myalgic encephalomyelitis (ME) / chronic fatigue syndrome (CFS). The years we'd spent pushing ourselves through twenty hour working days, chasing success and financial freedom by juggling multiple jobs, never allowing ourselves to rest even when we were sick, had evidently taken more of a toll than we'd realised. The best analogy one doctor gave was that her battery just didn't recharge like it should do anymore, with the root cause being a virus she'd suffered from in the past but hadn't fully recovered from. While I might go to bed exhausted after an especially hard day and wake up feeling completely refreshed after a good lie-in, Esther might now take days, or even weeks, to recover from the same exertion. Because there was no single 'treatment' the only way forward had been to make lifestyle changes. Esther had had to learn how to manage the condition with more stable routines and try to maintain baseline activity levels, such as regular getting up and going to bed times, for example.

35

In the motorhome we'd usually managed to bear this in mind, although there had been several bad relapses over the years since the diagnosis. Times when we'd gotten overexcited, done too much and been too busy for several weeks, if not several months, and Esther would need a period of almost complete bed rest to recover and ease back into a more stable routine. We'd chastise ourselves for being complacent, do our best to stick to her routines for a while, but unfortunately we still had a tendency to take our bodies too much for granted and get complacent again over time. The sort of complacency that would see us setting off on a four-week hiking adventure, expecting to wild camp the whole way and with no real plan in place for either route or resting, for example.

While I was feeling impatient to start hiking, Esther was fighting a personal battle simply to get out of her sleeping bag. Unfortunately, stood outside feeling like a muppet as the other campers departed, I didn't know quite how bad she was feeling. Just that she was tired. I could definitely sympathise with that. I was aching all over as well and hadn't enjoyed sliding on my cold, damp clothes saturated with two days of sweat, suncream and insect repellent either.

So, I tried to wait quietly and be a gentleman by not disturbing her before she was ready, doing what I could to pass the time and keep warm. The valley around us was still beautifully lush and green and peaceful and I'd known worse places to pass the time. I paced up and down the access road, I walked laps of the tent, I stood on one leg, I stood on the other leg, I took some photos of the brightening valley around us, I removed the soaking outer tent and carried it uphill to dry in a patch of sun and, once it was evident Esther was awake but just not getting up, I even leaned in and packed up my own air mattress and sleeping bag. Eventually, when all other avenues seemed exhausted, I began to indulge in self-pity. It wasn't fair that I was stuck outside on my own like this. What had I done wrong to be

36

ignored in this way? Weren't we supposed to be doing this adventure together? Why were we even doing this sodding hike in the first place if it was going to be like this? "Take your time, there's no rush, everything's fine" I kept saying, although in the end what I actually wanted to shout was "get up and stop moping you lazy git".

Esther did eventually emerge at around 9 a.m., the same time that the sun arrived in the valley floor, and the tension that had been silently building between us eased a little. According to Paddy, immediately ahead of us lay an 8 kilometre stretch containing a mere 300 metre climb to Pas de la Bosse, followed by an 800 metre descent into La Chappelle d'Abondance that would take around 2 ½ hours. After that all bets were off. With this relatively late start I could already feel my intention to crack on with 'Day 3', another 21 km epic involving almost 1500 metres of climbing, slipping away. It was making me cranky.

The previous day we had set out from our teepee smiling and full of optimism. Today we set out feeling slightly distant and melancholy. Almost symbolically a heavy mist materialised from the previously clear air just as we started going uphill, blocking out the sun and dropping the temperature straight back to the pre-dawn chill. As we climbed our conversation became increasingly one-sided, with Esther reeling off what I couldn't help hearing as a list of complaints aimed directly at me. "Our packs are just too heavy", "these stages are just silly", "we need to give more thought to how you access toilets", "I feel so dirty", "it can't stay like this for the next 4 weeks".....and so it went on. In hindsight, she just needed to feel heard after a rough start to the day. It was a time to listen and be sympathetic, maybe even agree that we'd been underestimating the hike and overestimating our bodies a little. At the time, however, I just wanted to try and make the 'problems' go away. Yet when it became clear that my 'helpful' suggestions, such as "well, why don't I carry your water bottles and the first aid kit as well then", weren't helping I lost my temper instead.

"Why do you have to be so fucking negative all the time" I shouted. It escalated from there.

It was a short, flash-in-the-pan argument and ultimately a very productive one. There were raised voices, some swearing, a few tears and, in the end, mutual agreement that things did indeed need to change slightly. We needed to focus more on our personal well-being instead of adhering to some arbitrary schedule written by the kind of person who would call the previous two days "longer but easier". We also needed to actually commit to being hikers, not tourists or backpackers, if we were really going to enjoy this adventure. Why exactly were we carrying trainers to go jogging, a yoga belt and extra smarter clothes if hiking was what we had come to do? Thanks primarily to our little flare-up, we acknowledged that our lack of commitment to a specific activity had caused us extra, unnecessary suffering.

By the time we started climbing again not only had the mist vanished, the mood had lifted too. We soon reached the top of the 300 metre climb to be greeted by some very friendly cows, who cheered us up even further, and then it was just the long descent into La Chapelle d'Abondance to go. The terrain was pleasant and green, still mostly made up of rolling hills covered with large swathes of trees and a handful of mossy crags that were quite reminiscent of the Lake District. If it wasn't for the abundance of marmots on display we might have imagined we were on a long descent into Patterdale from the top of High Street.

La Chapelle d'Abondance turned out to be a small village with plenty of accommodation options and we decided to go no further. Following our recent resolution to make some small changes to how we were approaching this adventure, we decided that Paddy could sod off until tomorrow. It was going to take us three days after all to do his 'Day 1' and 'Day 2' and that was that. Also, in a departure from our historic tendency to go as cheap as possible (i.e. camping, for free if we could), we decided to take a room. Well, I say decided, but after the previous two days it felt a lot like a physical necessity. It was the reason we were about to go against our natural instinct not to spend a penny more than we absolutely had to, at least not to alleviate personal discomfort anyway.

Choosing to exist in as challenging conditions as possible, rather than use a little of our savings in return for some comfort, was an egoic shadow we both had and it came from several places. Many years earlier, as students, we'd only had a tiny budget for our summer adventures and so counting every euro cent had been a financial imperative. Later, once we'd started working and earning, we'd both felt safer continuing to live as frugally as possible, especially as we had such big debts hanging over us. It helped that we were both natural savers. As a teenager I was the sort of kid who put aside my £5 paper round money for three months to save up for my own roller blades, a stark contrast to my brothers who would usually give their wages straight back to the newsagent in return for sticky treats. More recently, we both felt that the only reason we could even afford to travel as we were came down to the frugal life we'd led for the previous decade, saving, paying off mortgages and reducing our debts as fast as we could. It was a hard habit to deviate from.

Also, not only did it feel financially extravagant to pay for a room when we 'could' have managed without one, we also felt that by paying for a room we would be failing somehow. That we were weak and not doing it right. The image I had of 'real' long distance hikers was of hardy souls who only wild-camped and only washed in streams, not people who went for jolly strolls from place to place with their credit card on hand to bail them out whenever the going got tough. That was tourism, not living in the wild. Especially not after just 2 days!

However, as much as it was an ego-bashing moment on several levels to concede that a room was needed, there

39

was no doubt that it was the case if we wanted to stay sane and balanced as a couple. Denying ourselves comfort simply to prove that we could cope without it and keep our savings untouched, which we had done so many times in the past, was not happening today.

Thanks to an incredibly helpful tourist office, by late-afternoon we had found our way to Ferme La Fêto just off the main road, who had offered us a smart double room, ensuite, for 60 euros in a lovely Alpine style building. As the procession of hay bales past our window and the banging above our heads testified, it was very much a working farm, which added to the charm. Even I had to admit to myself that it was everything I had hoped to find and it felt awesome to shed our packs, close the door and step into the bliss of a private shower. It had only been just over 48 hours since we'd tentatively walked out of Thonon-les-Bains with little clue what lay ahead, but it felt so good it could have been 48 days. The shower paled into insignificance compared to the mattress though. Peeling back the crisp, clean white sheets and sliding my showered self between the smooth covers, with the springs gently supporting all of my aching bits and pieces, felt like I was being caressed by silk all over my body. Heaven.

After an afternoon nap we set out on a successful foraging expedition at the small local supermarket, resulting in us feasting on a whole sack of oranges, an entire watermelon and a lovely salad salsa with avocado that Esther had made. In the space of just a few hours we had washed, dozed and, finally, eaten away the trials of the trail. It was incredible how one day could contain such extremes of emotion. Internal ego battles about paying our way out of discomfort would just have to wait for another day to get resolved. "Pass me the salad bowl again please Esther...."

Vital Statistics - Day 3
Start: Chalets de Bise
End: La Chapelle d'Abondance
Distance Hiked: 8 kilometres
Hiking Time: 2.5 hours
Height Gain: 300 metres
Height Loss: 800 metres

6. Lightening The Load

A wonderfully comfortable night's sleep followed by a surprisingly tasty breakfast saw in the beginning of our fourth day on the trail. Usually our personal food choices make most of the options available in hotel breakfasts out of bounds. Well, not this morning!

By the way, just to be clear although I expect you've probably worked it out by now, Esther and I tend to eat a mostly plant-based diet. Don't worry though, I don't intend to get sanctimonious about personal food choices. It would be hypocritical for a start since up until about 6 or 7 years ago I was a card-carrying carnivore myself, ridiculing vegetarians by waving my barbecue mockingly in their general direction. "You don't know what you're missing" I would taunt through a mouthful of burger. The suggestion that I'd one day choose not to eat meat myself would have been about as realistic back then as the suggestion that I'd willingly cut off my man-bits with a rusty axe (I haven't done this by the way).

More importantly, however, I believe that the best way to enact and inspire change in the world is to passionately embody the change you'd love to see in others, not to harangue them and criticise their personal choices. We already live in a world of information overload, 24-hour media and 'alternative facts', a world where almost any statement can be backed up by so-called 'evidence', a world where opinions often get so entrenched that people starts throwing rocks at each other. The last thing people need, while going about their already busy lives, is to get stopped in the street to be told "you're doing it wrong".

That's not to say we should keep quiet about issues we happen to be passionate about for fear of upsetting people. Just that it's possible to be compassionate and gentle and to disagree without fighting. That way, when personal circumstances motivate someone to consider looking at something in a different way, they will know who they can talk to without fear of getting an "I told you so" for their trouble.

For us, changing the way that we ate was motivated, initially, by a period of especially high work stress and some correspondingly poor health. Esther was just 26 years old when she started getting severe chest pains and dizzy spells, something her GP immediately wanted to treat with high blood pressure medication. At the time we were trying to start our own business while also working full-time day jobs and were eating what we only semi-jokingly called the "pizza and cheesecake diet", with cheesecake being a catch-all term that included chocolate, donuts, pastries, cakes and any other sweet treats that took our fancy while we raided the supermarket. Frankly, it shouldn't have been surprising what the end result of eating so much junk was, especially for two apparently intelligent graduates, but we were young and used to our bodies dealing with anything. Esther's chest-pains were just the final straw that gave us a kick up the backside to make a change.

Because we'd both done a lot of sports we thought we already knew enough about healthy eating, but we went on to learn a lot more. We'd always believed in the mantra of "everything in moderation", but it's amazing how 'moderation' had crept up on us until the 'treats' had become the staples.

I don't want to get too technical about it, because it's unnecessary, but in short we just started eating a lot more unprocessed whole-foods, fruit and veg'. This wasn't some overnight change either, it was something we phased in over time by experimenting with new recipes and new ingredients. It was fun, it felt easy and it worked. We lost weight, Esther's dizziness and chest pains vanished along with her eczema and we had more energy. It was like we were different people and all we'd done was slowly cut out the junk and put some good fuel in our tanks. It sounds like a miracle (i.e. bollocks) to put it so simply but that's really

43

how it was. This wasn't some fad diet either, one where we had to spend so many days a week hungry, it was just eating lots of high nutrient food at every meal. It wasn't rocket science, we'd just needed a shock to push us in the right direction and stop treating our bodies like waste recycling centres.

Because we were cutting out so much junk, it was no surprise that we were feeling healthier. But what did surprise me was the speed of the improvement and the fact that as we added in more plant-based foods we also found ourselves gradually cutting out foods I never would have imagined being able to live without. Foods I had spent my whole life believing were 'essential' to both health and satisfaction at mealtimes. Meat, then fish and, a while later, other animal derived foods like dairy as well. I mean, after a while I was choosing not eat cheese for crying out loud and I wasn't missing it. I'd loved cheese even more than meat!

It was a virtuous cycle. The more plant-based foods we ate, the better we felt and the more we wanted to choose them over our old diet, and so it continued. I'm not saying anything new here by the way, I just wish that more people would try it for just 2 weeks so they could see what I mean.

It was only after a few years that the ethical side of not eating animal foods started to creep into my awareness and, after checking just a few facts about modern food production methods, quickly became an equal (if not greater) justification for steering away from them. It wasn't just the animal suffering but also the environmental degradation arising from intensive 'meat' production. Now that I'd learned I could be happy, healthy and thrive without those foods, I could no longer justify eating them, not even in small quantities.

Which is why, in the country of Camembert, foie gras and saucisson and where most natives go hiking with a 3-foot baguette strapped across their pack, we chose to haul beans, nuts, seeds, fresh fruit and vegetables across the mountains instead. It might seem difficult in the land of the

44

butcher, the baker and their rotund friend, the cheesemaker to source enough fresh, plant-based food to fuel several weeks living in the mountains, but it turned out to be much easier than we thought it would be with a little forward planning and a little trust that what we needed would be available, such as at Ferme La Fêto on the morning of our fourth day.

We had tried to turn down breakfast during check-in the previous afternoon, assuming that it would consist of the usual fare of bread, pastries, cheese and cold cuts of meat. "Oh, don't worry about us" we had said in our best French. However, opting out of being looked after was apparently not an option at Ferme La Fêto and so, on the friendly insistence of the owner, we had eventually said that "just some fruit" would be perfect. I expected an apple and a banana on a plate. What we got instead was a beautifully sliced and creatively presented feast of melons, grapes, apricots, plums and banana alongside a plethora of herbal teas arranged on a giant wooden platter. It was amazing.

A short while later we set off, pausing briefly at the post office to ship more than 4 kg of unnecessary baggage back to the UK. After our shaky start the previous day we had resolved to jettison everything that wasn't essential for a hiking adventure. Gone were the 'smart clothes' and trainers, the yoga belt, the water filter pump (since we were also carrying a UV Steripen with back up chlorine dioxide tablets to sterilise suspect water), 'spare' tent pegs, the gas burner ring (since we preferred the methylated spirits burner we were also carrying) and a bunch of other spare technical clothes. We'd also relieved our packs of the two glass jars of green powder we liked to use at home, decanting the powder into a ziplock bag and so instantly getting rid of another half a kilo. Feeling slightly silly not to have been more committed to this business of long distance hiking sooner, but excited to have now taken the plunge, our packs were noticeably lighter as we began the day's long march.

The only other stop we made was at the local store, where we picked up a cucumber and some oranges to supplement the dried food we expected to be cooking until we passed through another village in two days' time. Reasoning that the cucumber and oranges were essentially water bottles with a few added vitamins, we simply reduced the amount of fresh water in our packs accordingly.

Paddy's 'Day 3' outline, which we had also jointly resolved to treat as guidance rather than gospel from now on, suggested covering 21 km, climbing 1495 metres and descending 545 metres to reach the mountain refuge at Chésery, just across the border in Switzerland. Apparently, this would take Paddy 8 hours. Our new attitude was to just see how we got on, especially since our lovely, leisurely breakfast and time in the post office and store had meant we weren't setting out until midday again.

Certainly, the initial 900 metre climb out of La Chapelle d'Abondance was much easier going with our lighter packs and the weather remained settled and warm, although still overcast. The climb we were undertaking was essentially up and over the eastern shoulder of the 2432 metre Mont de Grange, but due to the thick forest which surrounded most of the route we didn't see much except tree trunks for most of the 3 hours it took. After what felt like a surprisingly short time we reached the 'top' at Les Mattes which, despite being at 1930 metres altitude, turned out to be a flat plateau with a chalet and a field of cows chewing the abundant, thick grass.

In fact, despite being close to 2000 metres altitude, most of the nearby terrain remained lush and green with plenty of trees on the slopes, although there were signs that would soon change as we continued south. Ahead of us we could now make out the snow-capped peaks of Dent Blanches, Dents du Midi and Mont Blanc beckoning us onwards. Apart from that single, fleeting glance of Mont Blanc on our second day, this was our first sight of the really high mountains that lay ahead.

A short and mostly gentle 200 metre descent followed, taking us into an area of more cows, ramshackle farmsteads and rocky access roads that would make up the majority of the trail for the next few hours. It was now coming up to 5 p.m., so we took a pause for a tasty dinner of black bean pasta with miso seasoning to fill our increasingly demanding tummies. It was while we were sat boiling up this feast, in the awkwardly small 1200 ml titanium pan we were sharing, that we got our first (and last) meeting with a GR5 hiker going the other way and therefore nearly finished! He was an older gentleman, heavily tanned and as lean as a whippet, who approached quickly before stopping abruptly to ask if there were any good wild camping spots nearby. He explained that he'd left Nice three weeks earlier and wanted to get to Geneva in two days' time, but was ready to put his head down for the evening. We wished him well, suggesting the fields of Les Mattes (as long as he didn't mind cows) and with a cheery 'Bon Appetit' he vanished as fast as he had appeared.

For us there was still around 3 hours of walking needed to reach Paddy's suggested overnight stop, which turned out to be pretty easy going. First, we got to enjoy an hour and a half of pleasant ambling along wide and almost flat access roads to reach the next milestone at the Col de Bassechaux, where we took another short break to appreciate the sweeping views. Then it was just another hour and a half on gradually climbing tracks to reach the Col de Chésery at 1992 metres. This was an exciting moment. Not only was this the new highest point of our hike so far, but it was also the point at which we would temporarily leave France and return to Swiss pastures.

The 'official' overnight stop was a refuge just a few hundred metres across the border, but we had no reservation and were still feeling relatively refreshed after spending the previous night in a real bed, so we decided it was time to get the tent out again. Even after 8 hours of hiking we still felt in a great mood and were even excited about spending our second night under canvas. Taking the room the night before had, if anything, increased our desire to wild camp. Also, at just under 2000 metres, this would be our highest night of wild camping ever.

A smattering of drizzle had blown across the trail during our final half an hour of walking but it had passed through by the time we got our tent out and set about the brief business of blowing up mattresses and unfurling sleeping bags. Prior to leaving the UK it had been several years since we'd camped wild, the last time being a single night trip in the Lake District, but it was a routine that was coming back gratifyingly quickly.

It also dawned on us that after spending 3 frustrating days feeling like we were chasing a tireless ghost, that we had stuck almost bang on to the suggested timings all day without really noticing. Perhaps Paddy wasn't so bad after all. Perhaps it was only us that had needed to condition up a little, shed a few kilos and approach the day with a more positive outlook.

Perching on some nearby rocks and firing up our stove to prepare a supper of more black bean pasta, we donned our down jackets and sat outside for as long as the deepening cold allowed while watching the ever-changing rainbow sky. Silhouettes of distant peaks emerged from the haze for just a short time as the sky darkened, and then all but vanished against a now moonlit sky. It was time to retreat to the relative warmth of our tent. We'd seen so few other hikers on our route so far that in this green, silent and still world we could almost believe we were the only people left at all.

Vital Statistics - Day 4
Start: La Chapelle d'Abondance
End: Col de Chésery
Distance Hiked: 21 kilometres
Hiking Time: 8 hours
Height Gain: 1495 metres
Height Loss: 545 metres

7. A Swiss Interlude

"Light you bastard", and other similar urgings, were some of my first thoughts on our fifth day of hiking. It was 2 a.m. and I was trying to light our Trangia meth's burner. I wasn't hungry. This was not an extreme attack of the midnight munchies, but I did need to heat up a litre of water so I could administer my first nocturnal enema of the adventure so far. I'd woken up aware of the familiar rumbling, unsettled feeling which confirmed that trying to postpone until morning would be a futile endeavour. Thankfully, despite my incredibly stiff muscles, I'd already managed to perform the complicated and cramped gymnastics required to wriggle myself out of both my sleeping bag and the narrow entrance to our tent without kneeling on Esther's head, shining my headtorch in her face or falling onto the inner tent and soaking my body with condensation. Now outside, I expect I cut a rather dashing figure in the moonlight wearing, as I was, an interesting ensemble of skin tight base-layer leggings, khaki hiking boots, a sky blue fluffy down jacket, orange headband and Esther's pink gloves. What can I say? I'm a fool for fashion.

There are a number of logistical problems to administering an enema outdoors, but the first one is always getting hold of some warm water. Once, many years earlier, Esther and I had slept in the back of our Citroen Picasso close to the Lake District village of Coniston. This was years before we considered a 'proper' motorhome and instead would remove the back seats from our car and sleep in the space normally reserved for shopping bags and shifting furniture. Waking up desperately needing the loo, we'd arrived in Coniston village at around 6 a.m. grateful to find the public toilet unlocked. I had no way of heating up water that morning and, unthinkingly, had filled up the water bag with the icy offering from the taps instead. It was a mistake I would only make once. Injecting a near frozen jet of water into my back passage had sent my internal plumbing into such an agonising spasm that I was unlikely to ever forget to use warm water ever again.

Back in the Alps and the problem I was having in the middle of the night, at a shade under 2000 metres, was that the methylated spirits in our Trangia burner was too cold. There just wasn't enough vapour to ignite. Since the only other source of warmth available was my body heat, all I could do was give it a cuddle to try and warm it up. It took twenty minutes standing in the cold with the sooty little burner nestled in my armpit before I managed to get it started.

Ten minutes later and I was stumbling away from the tent in search of a remote place to dig a hole that was also a good distance from the main trail. It's incredible how different a landscape can look in the dark. Illuminated by my head torch the rolling terrain, dotted with boulders of varying size, could have been the surface of the moon, or at least it could have been if the moon was covered in damp grass.

By the time I was finished I'd been outside for almost an hour, half of which I'd spent with my trousers down, and I was getting pretty cold. I yearned to go back to my sleeping bag. However, I always find it impossible to know if I'm entirely empty after an enema. Up here on the dark starlit mountainside, the thought of negotiating the narrow entrance to our tent a second time followed by a reversed performance of the gymnastics required to manoeuvre myself into a sleeping position was daunting enough. The possibility that I might then suddenly need to get up again, therefore, was just too much to risk. So, I passed more time admiring the moon and stars and jogging up and down the trail trying to keep warm. It really was a very beautiful night. With my head torch turned off so that my eyes could adjust to the dark, I began to discern the silhouettes of the hills picked out against the backdrop of stars sweeping across the sky. It was a magic moment and a sight I felt very grateful to be enjoying. I felt closer to nature in that moment than I had for a long time.

My second start to the day came at 7 a.m. when our alarm told us it was time to get moving. We always try to be mindful, when wild camping by a hiking route like this, that an early start is part of the deal. We may have had a small and relatively inconspicuous dark green tent but that didn't mean we needed to be part of the scenery for other visitors. Two days earlier, at Chalets de Bise, we had been on a semi-permitted area close to other buildings but here we were in an otherwise empty wilderness. Getting going early was, as we saw it, a common courtesy.

We also had another potentially long day ahead, with a suggested 25 kilometre stage to the town of Samoëns, involving 670 metres of ascent and 1940 metres of descent, on the cards. Another 7 hours of hiking. Not that we were put off by this I hasten to add, especially after breezing through 8 hours and sticking to Paddy's timings the previous afternoon. I suppose we really should have known better when we noticed that Paddy had added the reassuring words "despite the length, the distance can be covered fairly quickly and easily", but we really did feel that our conditioning was improving and it was mostly downhill. Surely this would be a straightforward day?

A dense and cold mist blew in as we packed our gear in the damp morning air, leaving our fingers like icicles trying to operate the various straps, ties and laces required to get ourselves underway. It didn't dampen our enthusiasm though, which remained charged with the thrill of having woken up close to 2000 metres altitude with not a soul around. If anything, the reduced visibility made us feel even more energised, like explorers in a new and uninhabited world, which in our own little way we were.

Just a few minutes of walking later and our bubble of isolation was popped as we reached Refuge de Chésery and met a handful of overnight guests also preparing for a day of hiking. We paused just long enough to refill our water bottles, stood next to the first patch of snow we had encountered so far, and were soon underway again, skirting the fringe of Lac Vert where an industrious mother duck was shepherding her fleet of six young ducklings. She had certainly chosen a stunning nursery for her little ones, with picturesque green hillside surrounding this calm patch of water on all sides. Leaving the shore behind it was only gently upwards towards the new high point of our journey so far, 2099 metres at the Portes de l'Hiver.

Now, according to Paddy, on a clear day the view from this particular notch in the landscape towards the glaciated flanks of Dent Blanches is stunning. Personally, we thought it was probably even further enhanced by the low clouds that were blowing quickly through the valley ahead of us, revealing only brief and tantalising snatches of the snowy mountain tops. It was more mysterious and wild.

After a short pause to appreciate the lushness of the Swiss landscape, or at least the parts that we could see, we started moving again along good and well signed tracks that led first downhill to La Pierre then upwards to the Col de Coux, where we would return to France. Having seen no more than two or three hikers since Refuge de Chésery, but countless bell-laden cows chewing the cud alongside their young calves, it was quite a surprise to find so many hikers and cyclists gathered at the col when we arrived. From the sound of it we had joined a summit of many nations, with French, German, Italian, English, Spanish and various other languages we couldn't place wafting through the air. Everyone had at least one thing in common though. Like us, they all seemed to have lunch on their minds.

Tucking out of the cool breeze alongside a small crowd sheltering against the now deserted customs post I fired up our Trangia, far more easily than the last time, and set about preparing some red lentils. We had arrived at the col beneath cloudy skies, keeping warm only by the effort of walking, so it was a relief that the clouds chose to vanish at almost the precise moment that our lunch was ready, allowing us to eat in peace beneath a warm sun while appreciating the awesome views from this remote border crossing. We even took the time, while our lentils went down, to dry our sodden tent and so lighten our load for the remaining four hours of walking still ahead of us.

It was early afternoon by the time we got underway again, quickly negotiating the 500 metres downhill and 250 metres back uphill that was required to reach the Col de la Golèse. As beautiful as the scenery was, frankly, it was mostly a relief to get this part out of the way. Here in a place only accessible on foot, with magnificent rocky ridgelines strung out across the horizon, our main concerns were that the weather was growing uncomfortably warm and that our legs were starting to tire noticeably. We'd arrived at the Col de Coux feeling great, but resting in the warm sun with a full belly had not quite had the restorative effect we had hoped for. Quite the opposite in fact. Mercifully, we thought, from the Col de la Golèse at least it was downhill all the way to Samöens and the end of the day. A brief glance at the altitude profile for the remainder of the stage seemed to imply it would be nothing more than a gentle, albeit long, plod.

Well, apparently not. After crossing the Col de la Golèse the reality of the subsequent 10 kilometre, almost 1000 metre descent was definitely not gentle. The paths largely consisted of relatively busy and rocky access roads at a gradient not quite steep enough to get the descent out of the way but just steep enough to be uncomfortable. With our sweaty feet pressed hard into the edges of our boots and our thighs burning with each step, it felt like it would never end. The afternoon heat, which by now had built even further, also wasn't helping and there wasn't even a decent view or a breath of wind due to the thick trees surrounding most of the trail. Then, to top it all off, there was even a small uphill section thrown in, which hadn't been on the profile, just to rub salt in the wound. Thoughts of our peaceful lunch seemed like a distant memory as we found ourselves taunted by that reassuring guidebook phrase, "despite the length, the distance can be covered fairly quickly and easily". It took us 3 hours to complete that descent.

You can often gauge our mood on a hike by how many photos we take. In good times we're snap happy. Some days we take literally hundreds of pictures. On our descent into Samöens we took one, a blurry snap of my sweaty back vanishing into some thick bushes just before we reached the town, which sort of sums up that section of the trail.

Samöens turned out to be far larger and busier than we expected. The pavements of the numerous streets were heaving with jostling tourists, while plenty more were browsing the various outdoor stores and souvenir shops or occupying the many cafes and restaurants. I wasn't interested in sightseeing though. Just as with our arrival in La Chappelle d'Abondance two days earlier, after that relentless descent it was finding a place to sleep that dominated my thoughts. And, just like in La Chappelle d'Abondance, I could feel my urge to get clean and horizontal on a comfy mattress arguing with my purist, hiker-man ego which was still saying things along the lines of.... "go and camp you softy, or aren't you tough enough? That's what a real hiker would do. OK, so you had a wobble a couple of days ago. Don't let it turn into a habit. Don't just throw money at the problem and get a room every time you get the chance. A real hiker would 'man-up' and so should you". This suffer-seeking side of my ego was further emboldened by the fact we had now carried our expensive hiking gear for an extra two days over the mountains. "Why are you carrying all this fancy hiking equipment if you aren't going to use it at every possibility you softy?" it teased.

Our recurring, inherent reluctance to spend money on creature comforts, instead of "pushing on", was then intensified further when it turned out that rooms in Samöens were in seemingly short supply and therefore noticeably more expensive than in La Chappelle d'Abondance. After queuing in the busy tourist office, it turned out we basically had three options. The first was to fork out close to 100 euros on a basic room for the night somewhere in town. The second was to walk several kilometres in the wrong direction, i.e. not on the GR5, to the nearest campsite. Or, the third was to "just keep walking" on the GR5 until we found somewhere to stay for less money, or pitched our tent in a quiet field. In our tired, sweaty state we felt paralysed by these options. None of them sounded especially attractive as we struggled not to focus more on the negatives than the positives. "How much?" "How far?" "What if we don't find anywhere.....?" Eventually, frustrated by our own indecision, we decided we could at least solve a simpler problem first and then work out where we were going to sleep.

The simpler problem was hunger and, more specifically, hunger for fresh food. While other hikers might have craved a cold beer, the hot and dehydrating descent into town had left me musing on melons and daydreaming of succulent oranges like never before. We left the crowded tourist office and set off in search of sustenance, which we expected would be easy, but what we didn't expect was that we would strike gold and stumble upon a well-stocked organic supermarket. Jackpot!

Ok, so I know I've already waffled on once about our food choices once already. I also know that, like most things food related, the organic vs. non-organic debate is mired in contradictory opinions. "It's good for you", "it's not worth the money", "it's good for the planet", "they just put an extra sticker on it even though it's the same stuff"....blah, blah, blah. Sometimes it feels like you could go insane trying to dig through the lies, half-truths and biased reporting (from both sides) surrounding this topic.

For us, based on our own (fairly extensive) reading of the official legislation surrounding organic farming and having spent time working closely with a Professor of Organic Agriculture in my previous job, Esther and I had made a commitment several years earlier not just to eat more plant-based foods, but also to buy organic when we could, reasoning that every little bit of consumer choice helps. When you buy a product, you vote for that product and what it stands for. We don't drink, smoke or spend money on expensive meals out and at the time we were even struggling to pay for a hotel room when we really needed one. However, choosing to use our money to support a move away from monoculture farming and intensive use of synthetic fertilisers was something we were comfortable with, and still are. We know that the organic certification system is far from perfect, but it still marks a step in the right direction. This commitment was further reinforced when we spent 3 months working on an organic farm during our motorhome travels and we experienced first-hand the increased labour and time required to avoid pesticides and other conventional fertilisers.

Anyway, back in Samöens, the fact that we had stumbled across an organic supermarket stocking not only organic fruit and veg' but also ingredients which are hard to find in mainstream chains was very exciting. Plus, as luck would have it, the store also happened to be directly opposite a 3-star hotel which we hadn't seen listed in the tourist office. Reasoning that it couldn't do any harm to at least ask I decided, while Esther stocked up on supplies, to pop over the road to check their prices and availability.

Less than an hour later and we were enjoying a feast on the balcony of our comfy room at Le Gai Soleil before heading down to the pool for a pre-bed swim and jacuzzi. It had been the 30-euro walk-in discount that had swung it. Yes, the first few seconds after handing over 80 euros still felt like this was an expensive way of giving up, but later on that evening, as we bubbled around in the hotel jacuzzi, that feeling had eased significantly.

More than anything, it was just nice to have made a decision and so not have to agonise over what we were going to do a moment longer. We really were our own worst enemies at times, making things far more complicated than they needed to be with our preconceptions of how things 'should' be and how we 'ought' to be doing things. This was our adventure after all. There was no right or wrong way to go about it... "just switch the bubbles on again will you Esther.....thank you.....ah, lovely".

The day had started with a lonely enema on a moonlit hillside. A couple of hours earlier I had been feeling hot, dazed and confused descending a seemingly never-ending slope. Now I was enjoying an outdoor whirlpool beneath a clear Alpine sky, overlooking mountains with an organic fruit and vegetable feast filling my belly.

What a day of contrasts.

Vital Statistics - Day 5
Start: Col de Chésery
End: Samöens
Distance Hiked: 25 kilometres
Hiking Time: 7 hours
Height Gain: 670 metres
Height Loss: 1940 metres

8. Just Keep Walking

In what looked like becoming a habit, as in both Thonon-les-Bains and in La Chapelle d'Abondance, we lingered for as long as possible in our room before re-joining the GR5. In a most un-hikerly fashion we enjoyed another pleasant lie-in, a leisurely pre-breakfast swim and jacuzzi and, finally, a long, hot shower that had us checking out (once again) only minutes before the official kicking-out time. Even then we didn't set off right away. The hotel had very kindly agreed to assist us in preparing an organic fruit and vegetable smoothie for our breakfast, a common feature of our diet back home and something we felt our weary bodies could benefit from, if we could only get our hands on one.

In practice this involved Esther nipping over the road to the organic supermarket after we'd checked out and returning with a bag containing avocado, lettuce, cucumbers, celery, apples, stem ginger and various other green things which, we explained to the reception staff, we would just like blended all together. Not quite what we normally did at home but it was at least easy to explain and, we hoped, wouldn't take too long for them to make. We weren't completely unaware that we still wanted to get a little walking done.

It turned out to be a longer wait than we had hoped for. As we sat I imagined our eclectic bag causing some confusion in a kitchen used to croissants, jam, pancakes and cold cuts of cheese and meat. I pictured a tall-hatted French chef exclaiming "zee Engleesh want to eat what!" before arguing it was beneath his culinary skills to simply "blend eet all togezza", because of course we all know French chefs speak like this. What did the owner take him for? Surely, my imaginary chef would argue, it could so easily be sautéed with a little garlic and sprinkled with parmesan cheese to produce a little tart, which would be delightful.

In the end it took over three quarters of an hour before a large plastic mixing bowl containing two litres of green-brown sludge was carried, at arm's length, out of the kitchen along with two spoons. At the back of the room we were aware of the proprietor looking at us, probably wanting to see if we'd really eat such a visually unappetising concoction. We did, and we (mostly) enjoyed it too. The stem ginger floaters were a bit of a taste explosion, but we still made it to the bottom.

We knew it looked odd to most people that we were so determined to consume so many fresh fruits and vegetables every day, even while hiking in the mountains. Hell, it probably is odd. But for the reasons I've already explained, we just wanted to take every opportunity we could to load up on vitamins and minerals. It had been such a key component of us climbing out of our personal health rut years beforehand and it had remained a very important part of our lifestyle. Not that we couldn't go without, if necessary, it's just that we were happy to stretch the term 'necessary' a little.

Back in La Chapelle d'Abondance we had left the village with cucumbers and oranges in the tops of our rucksacks. Here in Samöens, with the anticipated rarity of another organic supermarket on our doorstep, we went one step further and left town with three chunky cucumbers, a couple of avocados and a small watermelon jammed into the roof our bags. Again, we reasoned, it was only like carrying special types of water bottles.

We plodded slowly out of town a little after midday. Paddy's suggestion for the day ahead was an apparently demanding 23 kilometre stage, with 1800 metres of climbing and 500 metres of descent, which would take a predicted 8 hours. The altitude profile for the stage hammered home that this would be no mean feat, revealing a flattish 10 kilometres followed by steep climbing the rest of the way. Even with our happy, smoothie filled tummies and jacuzzi massaged muscles it was a daunting prospect.

The opening kilometres did indeed prove to be very straightforward, following the line of a river where we got to wave at a flotilla of passing white water rafters, bravely drifting along the millpond surface. I don't know how much rafting was costing them in Samöens in late July, but I hope those customers got a discount.

After around an hour of gentle ambling we veered away from the more manicured fields and trails to enter the Gorges des Tines. Like a lost world in miniature, this narrow, mossy cut in the limestone landscape is negotiated with the assistance of some cables and laddered sections and was a magical diversion from our steady plod by the river. After the gorge came a little up and down walking through some forest until the route returned back to the riverside. After a total of two hours of hiking we were an impressive 65 metres higher in altitude than we had been in Samöens.

It's the nature of my enema routine that, even though I had used my kit just a few hours earlier in our room, sometimes I need to use it again not very long afterwards. Such was the case on this sunny afternoon, which was irritating for two reasons. First, I knew we had a very long way to go and, second, it looked like it would mean a daytime, outdoor enema, something I was very reluctant to do. Thankfully, Lady Luck was on my side. Just as I was beginning to consider which of the numerous large logs by the trail would form the most sheltered, comfortable and effective toilet seat, we stumbled upon a block of toilets in an apparently deserted camping ground. With the uphill hiking portion of the day about to begin, it proved to be the perfect spot to take a pause, do what I needed to do and make a dent in some of the watery fruit weighing down our packs as well. It's uncanny how what you need the most sometimes seems to appear out of nowhere.

We were on our way again by mid-afternoon and the trail immediately started heading uphill. The area we were entering into was a popular destination for day hikers, with several impressive waterfalls and a number of Alpine refuges that could be reached on a long day hike. The first hour or so of climbing had us alternating between forest tracks and the thin strip of tarmac which leads up to the Chalet de Lignon, where the road ended. Leaving the road behind, we then joined an ever climbing, forested path up the valley of the Torrent de Sales. We were climbing the eastern flank of the valley, which meant that we could see little on our left side except more trees rising far above our heads, but on our right we had amazing views of the towering wall of rock that made up the western flank. With countless threadlike waterfalls dispersing into misty smears over the twisted layers of rock, it was an impressive and slightly intimidating sight that made us aware of just how tiny we were in this gigantic landscape.

Late afternoon drifted into early evening as we climbed ever higher on the rocky and often steep paths. Along with the softening light came a deluge of day-hikers coming the other way. With clouds building it had the disconcerting effect of making me wonder if we weren't going in the wrong direction. Did they know something we didn't? Yet we continued onwards and upwards, nodding and bonjouring to each passing group.

The reward, when we reached the top of the climb at the Collet d'Anterne, after a total of 3 hours and 1000 vertical metres since our last and only break so far that day, was a majestic view back down the valley that we had spent the afternoon walking along and then up. Earlier in the day, when we had still been ambling along the flat banks of the river, we had stopped to refill our water bottles at a lodge. The occupant had asked where we were heading to and, when we'd responded that we were doing the GR5, he had proceeded to explain the route ahead in very rapid and detailed French. We hadn't been able to follow everything he said, but one thing that had stuck in our minds was the sight of a very distant and high-altitude pylon which he seemed to be saying we would pass beneath. "No way" we had thought. "That's way too high and far away. He must have misunderstood us." We were now stood directly beneath that pylon.

But there was little time to pause and savour the view. The day was wearing on and the clouds were darkening. We hastened on for another half an hour across an undulating landscape of shrubs, grass, crags and boulders and then up another short climb onto a green plateau. We had now reached the ramshackle looking cluster of buildings that make up the mountain refuge named after Alfred Wills, founder of the Alpine club.

By this point we weren't speaking very much at all, not because we'd had an argument, but in order to preserve our flagging energy. Esther was actually listening to exercise class recordings on her MP3 player just to keep herself going, with fast paced music and motivational classics along the lines of "......and you're nearly there, keep pushing, 2, 3, 4....". Poor timing really since we were not, in fact, nearly there at all.

It was almost 7 p.m. and, since we had just arrived at a mountain refuge, one of the main purposes of which is to provide shelter, we thought we might find someone to ask if we might camp nearby. Unfortunately, the few staff we could see were so busy serving fondue to the large number of guests sprawled around the picnic benches, that after almost quarter of an hour we still hadn't managed to speak to any of them.

Feeling exhausted, a little vulnerable and more than a little out of place alongside the cheese munching hordes at the refuge, we suddenly spotted what looked like several slow-moving blobs going uphill on the exposed looking climb ahead of us. It was a sight that prompted a snap decision. Yes, it was late. Yes, we were tired. Yes, it was a little bit scary and wild. But there seemed to be no joy for us at the refuge and technically, since it was a natural reserve, we knew wild-camping was forbidden anyway. As seemed to be our habit, having made no real plans, no prior arrangements and with no apparently better options, we decided to keep going instead. If those blobs above were still moving, why couldn't we?

So up and over we went, another 300 metres of climbing on a steep, zig-zagging path followed by a longer but more gentle descent to reach the surprisingly large and remote mountain lake of Lac d'Anterne. What a stunning location, set in a vast, shallow bowl of rock with countless threadlike tributaries feeding the still waters of the lake. We really felt like we were in the high mountains now, especially as the brooding sky made the location seem that much more wild and threatening. There was still plenty of snow on the crags around the rim of the bowl and even the tops of the imposing walls of rock, the same ones that we had craned our necks to look up at hours earlier, were now below us.

As we walked along the shores of the lake it was very tempting to pitch our tent right there and then. We wouldn't have been alone. Half a dozen other tents could be seen dotted around, including one particularly large heap of canvas belonging to an English family that we'd said hello to and who were trekking with a clutch of children and a donkey! It really was a beautiful location for camping and yet, having already come so far on Paddy's suggested itinerary for the day, there was a part of us that wanted to 'finish it'. There was just one more section of up and down to go. Just one more hour. We knew we could do it.

It was almost 9 p.m. by the time we reached the Col d'Anterne at 2257 metres. Just 250 metres below us we could now make out the twinkling lights of the refuge that marked the end of the stage, like a light at the end of a tunnel. It was both a very welcome and a very welcoming sight, but in the end we didn't quite make it. Instead, around ten minutes before reaching the refuge, we came across a patch of ground that just begged to be camped on. Not because it was flat, although it was. Not because it had a water source, although it did. Not even because it was quiet and sheltered, although it was both of these as well. The reason it begged to be camped on was because the summit of Mont Blanc had just emerged from the now dispersing clouds and this particular spot offered an unrivalled, unimpeded view across the miles of clear air between us and Europe's highest summit.

To be alone in the silent wilderness, watching the gold, then pink, then red light of the sunset play across that world-famous vista of snow, ice and rock was a chance we didn't want to miss. We pitched our tent, donned our down jackets and sat together watching as the clouds slowly vanished and the bulk of the Mont Blanc massif became completely visible.

We'd just hiked 23 kilometres, with 1800m of ascent and 500m of descent, in 9 hours and only taken a single stop, but all of the exhaustion was immediately washed away by the thrill of seeing the imposing mass of Mont Blanc looking so gigantic and close we could almost touch it.

Vital Statistics - Day 6
Start: Samöens
End: Refuge de Moëde Anterne (well, almost)
Distance Hiked: 23 kilometres
Hiking Time: 9 hours
Height Gain: 1800 metres
Height Loss: 505 metres

9. Hot, Hot, Hot

There were people everywhere I looked. Lounging on rocks, shuffling like sheep through the snow and, many of them, just standing around looking aimless. A few moments earlier we had been in blissful isolation, able to count on one hand the number of people we'd been close enough to speak to since waking up, and now there were thousands of them. Laughing, drinking, smoking, dropping litter, getting in my way and basically doing all of the other things that bother me at sea level, never mind at 2525 metres. What the chuff was going on? Had I slipped off the mountain and woken up in hell?

The morning, prior to this, had been wonderful. We'd woken up to the sight of a sun-dappled Mont Blanc winking at us across a crystal-clear sky. We'd descended, with a spring in our step, for 500 metres, down to the Pont d'Arlevé. We'd climbed solidly, for 3 hours and another 1000 vertical metres, drinking in the panoramic views as we approached the summit of Le Brévent. And then, just as we arrived at the top, we had stepped into some sort of folk concert, with throngs of people milling around to what sounded a lot like oompah-oompah music. Yep, definitely purgatory.

I was, of course, being grumpy. We really had enjoyed a great morning but now, unfortunately, I once again really needed to use my enema kit. The last thing I had expected to find at the summit of Le Brévent was thousands of people. I'd known that there was a cable car that came up from Chamonix but seriously, it must have been packed out like a Japanese commuter train at rush hour. Probably the vast majority of 2500 metre peaks across the globe are ideal places to shove a pipe up one's bottom in peace, but the summit of Le Brévent on a hot and sunny day in July is not one of them.

Don't get me wrong. Unlike some die-hard hikers, who declaim them as "scars on the landscape", I'm actually a fan of cable cars in general. I think it's great that people who happen to be less physically able, or who don't have the time to walk uphill for an entire day, get the chance to appreciate the beauty of nature in the very special way that being high up offers, provided they can afford the ticket prices anyway (which sadly are often obstructively high for single day-trippers). It's just that on this particular day, after not just three hours of walking uphill but also the best part of a week in mostly quiet wilderness, it was very jarring to suddenly find myself surrounded by a noisy horde set against some irritating background honking.

Also, not only was I unexpectedly hemmed in moments after being on an exposed cliff face, but a noticeable portion of the crowd were casually tossing cigarette butts, drinks tins, crisp packets and other litter into the snow. It was like watching someone take a crap on my personal happy place. Honestly, why come up here to this beautiful paradise and then act like you don't give a shit? I could feel the red mist starting to descend, my jaw clenched and I was ready to start thrusting the tungsten sharp tips of my carbon fibre hiking poles into the eye sockets of the next person that spat across my path. In short, I was about to go Incredible Hulk, albeit a 5 foot seven inch version with ginger hair.

Waddling and weaving through the shuffling crowds towards the cable car station, forcing myself not to kick anyone in anger or garotte them with my drinking tube, I was then further disappointed to find the few facilities on offer in commercial lockdown, with a purchase being necessary to access them.

Under less stressful circumstances I'd normally be happy to agree that if someone is going to provide toilet facilities at 2500 metres then why shouldn't they charge a small fee to access them. It probably helps to stop them getting overwhelmed and toilets don't fly themselves up mountains for free. On the other hand, I'm a passionate advocate for free access to toilets, particularly for people with special requirements. As with the question of cable cars, there is no absolute right and wrong here. However, in my now flustered state, I did get more than a little irate at the toilet situation I had stumbled into. In my opinion at the time, since these irritating crowds were only there because of the facilities and the crowds were also the reason I couldn't sort myself out in peace, I should have been allowed to access those toilets immediately! It was only fair.

Feeling paralysed and uncomfortable, being stuck close to so many people in my moment of need, it was an equally flustered Esther that I shoved forward to explain my circumstances to the harassed looking restaurant staff. It took a while to get their attention, but it turned out they were more than happy to let me use their toilets, for free if I wanted to. They didn't mind. "Go ahead" was their relaxed response as they waved in the direction of the relevant stairs. My judgemental grumpiness at the restaurant had been totally unfounded, and being told to "go ahead" in such a friendly manner was quite a humbling experience that helped to snap me out of my temper. There I'd been, arriving at the summit all puffed up with my own superiority because I had walked all the way when these other lazy, messy and noisy reprobates had taken the easy way, using this as some sort of basis for my having more rights than them, and this small act of kindness reminded me that we were all just people. All at the summit for a similar reason, to appreciate this unique and special view of Europe's highest mountain on a perfect day to see it. Except the tossers dropping litter of course. Nobs.

Speaking of the view, which I haven't mentioned yet because I've been too busy being grumpy, it was undeniably awesome! On a clear day, such as we had, this particular summit really was the perfect place from which to appreciate the full majesty of Mont Blanc and its sister summits strung out along the enormous massif. Everything seemed both enormous and tiny at the same time. Enormous, because we knew intellectually that everything we could see across the valley, the peaks, glaciers, waterfalls and landslides, were best measured in kilometres. Yet also tiny, because being able to see them all at once, to easily slot them into a single photograph, made it like holding a postcard. Because everything was on the same huge scale, nothing stood out as being especially gigantic. It was slightly disorientating, in a good way.

The spot we chose to eat at has to go down on record as perhaps the greatest table we've ever had. It's certainly in the top five, positioned as we were on a rocky outcrop that pointed directly across the gaping valley that separates Le Brévent from its much bigger neighbour. Where better to appreciate not one, but two saucepans of bean pasta. This was the very last of our food so we did consider keeping something back as an emergency ration, just in case we didn't make it to a shop by the end of the day, but I guess in the excitement of the moment combined with severe hunger since we'd barely eaten at breakfast, we threw caution to the wind and ate everything we had left all in one go. It was probably for the best. Without a decent meal we may not have made it off the hill by dark at all. Not that we were thinking of our now empty supplies at the time, we were just hypnotised by the view. There was just so much to take in that to focus on any one part of it, a crag, a crack in a glacier, a rock promontory, a snowdrift on a summit, was to lose the enormity of the whole. Far better to just sit back, lose focus just a little, and take in everything from the blue sky to the grey scree tumbling into the valley.

Despite the small business of a vertical mile of descending still ahead of us and despite having no shelter at all from the now blazing sun, we sat for well over an hour trying to imprint that view on our memory forever. Everything felt perfect, or at least it did until we tackled the descent anyway.

The 'small' business of descending a vertical mile turned out to be not such a small business after all. First, we zig-zagged across open mountainside, then through scrubby bushes and eventually along forested slopes, and it just seemed to go on and on and on. Just as with our descent into Samöens, the gradient was too steep to take it easy but not steep enough to get the descent over with quickly and so required thigh-burning, foot pinching control on almost every step for the entire three hours that it took us. Also, since this south face of Le Brévent had been in the sun for most of the day, by this point every surface was baking hot and we could feel the stifling, scorched air pressing in on us from all sides.

I knew almost as soon as we had left the top that we were going to run out of water before we reached the bottom. There had been no water source at the summit and, although we had forked out for a couple of alarmingly expensive and small bottles of water, which we'd drunk with lunch, it wasn't going to be enough. Being the idiot that I am, I decided to keep my own meagre ration in reserve for Esther and didn't drink at all for the entire descent. I lied that I was when she asked and then shared what I had left once hers was all gone, but even that didn't last the whole way. It really was foolish of me because if I had passed out from dehydration we could have both been in serious danger. It was also a reminder of how vulnerable we still were in this wilderness. Even though we were close to one of the busiest resorts in the French Alps. Even though there were thousands of people within a few kilometres of us. Even though we were just an hour or so from civilisation, all it took was one hot day and one dried up stream and we could have become seriously unwell.

By the time we stumbled into the town of Les Houches we were two very hot, very thirsty, very salty, very dusty and very relieved hikers. It was 5 p.m. and, even though we'd enjoyed 'that view' for most of the way down, all we could think about was water and some juicy, fresh food. Thankfully, all of our wishes were about to be granted when we stumbled upon another well-stocked organic supermarket within minutes of arriving in town. Heaven! We thought we'd hit the jackpot in Samöens and now, just 48 hours later, it had happened all over again.

A brief buying frenzy followed which left us sprawled on the grass verge in front of the shop downing several deliciously cooling bottles of fizzy kombucha (a fermented green tea drink we love, try it!) and inhaling several bags of frozen mango pieces. With our salt-encrusted clothes and dust streaked cheeks I half expected someone to toss us a few euro cents, despite the fact we were guzzling nature's organic bounty, but we soon began to feel more human again and went back inside to get our hands on more food for dinner.

No sooner had we quenched our ravenous thirst when the debate on where to consume the rest of our organic food haul unexpectedly turned a little fractious. The routine we'd fallen into so far had involved two days of hiking, with one night in the tent and one night in a room. For me, after the baking descent and also having had two room experiences already to help overcome my egoic desire to 'camp at all costs', I just wanted to do the same again. I really couldn't face the idea of putting up the tent and also, after my enema difficulties at the top, I really wanted a private shower and room to get myself straight in. Naturally Esther agreed, in principle, and so we began to look.

However, after spending an exhausting and fruitless hour walking up and down the streets of Les Houches, it looked like the only hotel with a vacancy for less than 200 euros, far more than we thought reasonable, was a lady offering what was literally a storage cupboard. It contained a single bunkbed suspended above a stack of toilet paper, a tiny shower stuffed full with mop buckets and cleaning products, and a foldaway bed that we just might be able to find space for. Our understanding was that staff occasionally napped there, but we could have it for the night, if we wanted, for the bargain price of 60 euros! Unfortunately, the pool had already closed. This was when we began to get tetchy. Not because the pool had closed, but because we couldn't reach agreement on what to do next.

By now I was just desperate to stop searching and so wanted to take the cupboard, jam my bag in the shower and fall asleep for 12 hours, regardless of how ludicrous it was for the money. I couldn't face the idea of more walking, putting up the tent, communal showers and wriggling about in my sleeping bag. Esther, correctly, felt it was still over-priced and that the campsite wasn't that far away at a cost of just 13 euros. We argued, and in our mutually exhausted and dirty state it got far more heated than it needed to. But, to cut a long story short, we ended up at the campsite feeling more than a little distant and irritated with each other.

In fairness, I should probably also add that we never felt that the lady with the cupboard was profiteering or trying to take advantage. This was still the Chamonix valley in the middle of the high season after all and she really was trying to help even though she was technically full. When we'd said "thank you but we're going to camp after all" she suddenly produced two free bus passes usually given to paying guests that saved us a kilometre of weary hiking to the campsite.

Despite my preference for a pocket-sprung mattress and duvet over my 60-centimetre-wide airbed and green fluffy sleeping tube, I have to say that the campsite in Les Houches was, unsurprisingly, everything we needed. Lukewarm showers, cold water sinks for washing our faces, 'bring-your-own-headtorch' toilet cubicles and our very own petite patch of grass to call home for the night. It even came with another stunning view, this time of the surrounding mountains that rose steeply out of the ground on either side of the narrow valley we were bedding down in. It was getting a little late by the time we got the tent set up and sat on the moistening grass eating our dinner of fresh salad vegetables and tofu in moody silence, watching the few clouds in the sky reflecting the colours of the sunset. Neither of us wanted to be the first to break the silence for fear we'd start arguing again, which was silly because neither of us wanted to do that after such an amazing day.

As usual, our little spat was over almost as soon as it began, but it proved to be a very productive little disagreement that turned into a bit of a heart to heart. On my part I admitted that, yes, I was still pretending that my enema requirements were easier to cope with than they really were out here in the wild. During the previous week, in addition to the various conventional toilet facilities I'd been able to find, I had given myself enemas in strangers' houses, on logs, on boulders, several times in the middle of the night and in a hot and crowded restaurant toilet on top of a mountain with a dozen people queuing outside. Not only that but, without wanting to be too graphic about it, because of the times when I'd had to struggle on a little longer than I would have liked, the skin on my bum and upper thighs was now cracked, red and sore. It actually had not been very easy at all to deal with, even if I had still been trying to shrug the whole thing off and act like the outdoor loving, super long distance hiker I wanted to see myself as. Turns out that bowel incontinence actually is a bit of an issue on long distance hikes. Who'd have guessed it?

We also agreed that perhaps we were still overdoing it a bit and even raised the question of perhaps taking a complete rest day. This was not a word that had previously entered our vocabulary. Partly this was due to perceived time constraints. It was now the 30th July and on the 21st August we would fly from Geneva to Cairo for our much-anticipated Egypt trip. Allowing 2 days to travel back to Geneva, to be on the safe side, that meant that we only had 20 full days of hiking time left. Since even Paddy's fastest GR5 itinerary took 29 days to reach Nice, of which we had completed just 6 so far, we were already 3 days short of time. Our thinking prior to going over Le Brévent was that

73

we needed to be pushing on to make up time, not easing off to 'rest', at least if we were going to complete the GR5 before it was time to fly.

It wasn't just time constraints that were driving us on though. We were well aware that we didn't *have* to make it all the way to Nice. We weren't meeting anyone there and, even if we were, could always take public transport for part of the way. But that still felt like failing somehow. That not making it to the place we hadn't even really committed to reaching, since we still occasionally chatted about other route options, would somehow be letting ourselves down. It made no logical sense, and yet we still felt reluctant to take a day off.

Vital Statistics - Day 7
Start: Refuge de Moëde Anterne (well, almost)
End: Les Houches
Distance Hiked: 21 kilometres
Hiking Time: 7 hours
Height Gain: 1000 metres
Height Loss: 1900 metres

10. You Can't Take It With You

Even though we had tentatively agreed to take a rest day and even though we had both admitted, much to our ego's annoyance, that our bodies were extremely ready for one, the actual rest day itself felt far too precious to waste sitting on grass in a breezy campsite. If recuperation was the objective then surely it would be much better achieved by getting another room somewhere, or at least that's what we thought anyway. Therefore, instead of staying put, at about 10 a.m. we got up, packed away our gear and swung our packs onto our bruised shoulders so that we could continue on the GR5. Naturally, rather than staying in the busy and apparently expensive town of Les Houches, we had decided to keep going for just another day or so until a better opportunity presented itself. But then, we promised ourselves, we'd have a rest. Probably. When in doubt, just keep walking.

And besides, today was going to be an easy one, with the guidebook suggesting just 17 kilometres with a meagre 1050 metres of ascending and 895 metres of descending to reach Les Contamines. Paddy even described it as "fairly easy walking, mostly along tracks and minor roads". You might think we'd have seen this as a warning sign by now, but we didn't. Compared to what we'd been doing for the last few days it certainly sounded easy enough and we knew, having visited Les Contamines during our motorhome adventures, that there were plenty of places to stay once we got there.

Before leaving Les Houches for good we made a final visit to the organic supermarket, partly to replenish our non-existent supplies and partly to have a lovely big breakfast. The breakfast part certainly went well, but the stocking up somehow went a little haywire. We'd set off from La Chapelle d'Abondance with a cucumber and some oranges, from Samöens with three cucumbers, some avocados and a watermelon, but this time we really went to town. Perhaps it was because we had gotten so hungry the previous day and our eyes were still bigger than our bellies. Perhaps it was because we were excited by how many of our personal favourite foods were on offer and couldn't stop ourselves. Or maybe we were scared that we wouldn't see some of these particular ingredients again this side of the Mediterranean. Maybe it was all of the above. Either way, by the time we actually left Les Houches, I found myself hauling a rucksack containing not only three cucumbers and a melon, but also more avocados, a kilo of carrots, a can of black beans, sunflower seeds, pumpkin seeds, a jar of sauerkraut, three packs of tempeh (a fermented tofu product), two types of rye bread, three types of bean pasta and some semolina. I know we'd set out with a fair amount of food from the UK but this was just silly, especially as we planned to reach Les Contamines by nightfall which definitely had a supermarket of its own, organic or not.

'Stocking up' whenever we got the chance had really become a habit during our motorhome adventure. It was something we enjoyed doing and at times had almost felt like a hobby. Wherever we went, if we spotted an organic supermarket, we'd head inside to browse. If we found a new product we thought we might like, we'd buy several packs. We'd also load up, in bulk, on staples and other foods we knew that we liked. Not only did it help to keep our costs down but we knew we'd never run out either. Most of the time three quarters of our motorhome storage space was filled with boxes of various long-life foods and powders and there were usually several extra shopping bags lying around containing stuff which didn't have a space yet. It wasn't that we *couldn't* shop at the larger, cheaper supermarket chains such as Carrefour, Lidl and Aldi, all of whom have introduced more organic food options in recent years, which is great. We just preferred supporting dedicated organic supermarkets, especially the smaller independent ones, wherever we could. Plus, like I said, it was kind of fun. And besides, although we usually had several months' worth of food on board, way more than we really needed, it was a diesel engine doing the work.

Unfortunately, here in Les Houches, the job of the diesel engine was about to fall upon my own weary shoulders and thighs. Not that I minded because I was secretly a little excited about how heavy my pack was. Despite our recent chats about doing things sensibly, part of me still wanted to be the tough guy carrying the heaviest pack in France. Or should that say the idiot carrying the heaviest pack in France?

By the time we began the surprisingly steep and uneven climb out of Les Houches towards the Col de Voza, I estimated that my pack had swollen to well in excess of 20 kg and was likely creeping towards 25 kg. It was definitely feeling heavier than it had back in Thonon-les-Bains and I was fitter and stronger now. "Much heavier than most packs being on the GR5" I thought, feeling quite impressed with myself. I even began winding Esther up a little bit about why we kept feeling the need to "take our cucumbers for a walk", mostly to draw attention to how strong I was being I suppose. Unfortunately, this then had the unexpected, knock-on effect of making her feel like I was genuinely complaining and blaming her for buying so much stuff, even though I was secretly enjoying my unnecessary battle with gravity.

Not for the first time I had now put myself in a lose-lose situation by opening my big mouth. Either I really was complaining, in which case I should have spoken up about the quantity of food being purchased while still at the shop, or I was just an idiot who had deliberately and foolishly agreed to overload his own rucksack to show strong he was and then realised it was too much. Oh, and then it started to rain. Here we were, already having agreed that we were knackered and in need of a rest day, but going up a surprisingly steep hill regardless with me wearing a pack that was unquestionably too heavy and now we were getting wet. Only 16 out of 17 kilometres still to go. Aren't egos wonderful? They act like they're your best friend yet they get you into all sorts of trouble.

The tension of the previous night was definitely starting to return as we each began to realise that, despite our uplifting heart-to-heart only hours earlier about not trying to do too much, we'd already gone and done it again. I honestly can't say who we were more annoyed at, ourselves or each other. Instead we struggled on in silence, our bodies leaning into the slope and our feet scratching out small steps on the loose stony surface which went ever upwards. What we needed was something to happen that would take our minds off of our aching muscles and our returning doubts about what we were even walking uphill for anyway. Something to bring us together again. Something to make us smile and remind us of the beauty all around us. And then it arrived, in the form of a petite friendly face beneath a headscarf and fringe of ginger of hair.

We met Rotem just before we reached the top of the Col de Voza, after almost 2 hours and 650 metres of steep ascent. She was an Israeli who was hiking for 4 days around the Tour du Mont Blanc, setting out from Chamonix and hoping to reach as far as Courmayeur, before travelling to a work placement in Germany for two months.

The Tour du Mont Blanc, or TMB for short, is Europe's most well known and most popular long-distance hiking trail, a 170 kilometre loop around Europe's highest mountain. Every year thousands of hikers set off to complete all or part of the tour, passing through France, Italy and Switzerland along the way and also, in doing so, completing a little bit of GR5 as well. Variants aside, the TMB and the GR5 share the same paths all the way from the Col du Brévent, just before the summit of Le Brévent, and the Refuge du Bonhomme, an Alpine refuge some 6 hours of hiking beyond Les Contamines. That's the better part of three days of walking.

Knowing this in advance, I had been a little concerned about congestion on the trail in this area. After enjoying such a peaceful first week I was worried that the shared TMB stages would be much busier and detract from the scenery somehow, but so far that had not been the case at all. Quite the opposite in fact, if our friendly interaction with Rotem was anything to go by. Having somebody new to chat to and get to know for the next couple of hours was fantastic fun, as well as effortlessly diffusing the tension between us as well.

The route after the Col de Voza wound slowly downhill, on good tracks, mostly through forest but with several stretches on quiet roads as well. There were also a few short climbs thrown in, but that was OK because it helped us to keep warm as the chilly mist and drizzle came and went. The view that we could see, beneath the clouds, was of a lush, green and tree studded valley. Prior to cresting the Col de Voza the uphill had seemed never-ending but with company the time just flew by.

I suppose, having only had each other to speak to for almost the entirety of the previous week, that having anybody new to speak to would have been a novelty, but Rotem also happened to be especially intelligent, funny and interesting. She told us about her job as a teacher in Israel, about the politics of her homeland, about the work she would be doing in Europe over summer and about her hopes and dreams for the future. We, in return, told her of our lives before setting off to travel and about how we tried not to make too many plans anymore, sometimes to our own detriment. Although we'd only just met, it was as though the shared objective of walking and appreciation of being in nature made the conversation far more open and flowing than it might otherwise have been. We talked like old friends meeting after a long absence. It was actually a very sad moment to part company at an otherwise nondescript trail junction, exchanging email addresses (the first of a collection we would build up during this adventure), as our destinations for the night weren't the same.

We'd been on the go for over four hours by the time we said farewell to Rotem, without a break and often in the rain, and the guidebook suggested we still had 2 hours to go to reach Les Contamines. Like a weight being put back on our shoulders, with Rotem's departure we suddenly remembered just how tired we were. Each step became a struggle against the urge to just stop, sit and stare at the clouds. With nothing better to do and nowhere plausible to pitch up for the night, we just about managed to plod on through more open fields and along minor roads until, passing through the hamlet of Tresse, we passed a sign in big letters that read "Chambres" (rooms).

A few years earlier we would never have stopped for such a sign, assuming it would either be too expensive or inconvenient, or both. We would have plugged on to our albeit arbitrary destination come what may. Yet today was different. Ever since our chat the night before we'd had the idea in the back of our minds that we had a tendency to try and do far too much, not just on this hike but in life in general, and the inadvertent and rather foolish overloading of my pack had been the straw that almost broke the camel's back (it certainly gave me the hump, get it?) Anyway, we said we'd rest in a room and here was a room, right on our path. Perhaps this was fate intervening?

Rapidly agreeing that a ballpark figure of around 60 euros was our upper limit for a night, Esther went inside to ask if there was space, returning moments later to say that there was only one room left and the cost, uncannily, was exactly 60 euros. We said yes immediately. It was like providence intervening in our masochism. The room turned out to be one of only three available in the home of a lady named Françoise Bouvet ("Call me Fan-fan") and was delightful. Lovingly and smartly furnished with a balcony and a large shared bathroom just across the hall, we instantly fell in love with it. So much so that after emptying our bags of damp gear, handwashing our filthy clothes and eating a dinner of some of the food I'd been hauling all day, we decided to book in for two nights right away so that we could nod off secure in the knowledge that we didn't have to move tomorrow. Not one inch. After 8 days of continuous trekking, we were going to get our rest day after all.

Vital Statistics - Day 8
Start: Les Houches
End: Tresse
Distance Hiked: 14 kilometres
Hiking Time: 4 ½ hours
Height Gain: 950 metres
Height Loss: 895 metres

11. Going Nowhere Slowly

As morning slowly dawned on the other side of the curtains I found myself lying half-awake, just conscious enough to bask in the cosy softness of the mattress and duvet wrapped around me, when I was struck by several of the happiest thoughts of my life. I didn't have to get out of bed. I didn't have to put on dirty hiking gear. I didn't have to pack away a tent with cold hands. I didn't even have to walk uphill, or downhill for that matter. My agenda for the day involved little more than breakfast, lunch, dinner and a bath. Yes, an actual bath, with bubbles. Oh, happy day.

Although I quite like to consider myself a bit of a 'tough guy, outdoor enthusiast', getting out camping, cycling and hiking and all that, come rain or shine, I am going to let you in on a little secret. I don't actually like being uncomfortable. Sometimes in the past, when I've been reading books written by folk like Bear Grylls climbing Everest or Andrew Skurka racing along the Appalachian Trail, I couldn't help wondering if such people actually like discomfort. Did they like being filthy for days on end? Did they thrive on it? Did it make them feel good about themselves?

Don't get me wrong, I understand the need to push boundaries and feel yourself at the edge. Running up and down mountains, seeking out steep hills simply to cycle over them, trekking along precipitous ledges. I love that kind of thing. I can't get enough of it, but I still like having a nice warm wash and a comfy bed to look forward to at the end of the day. I adore being alone in the wild with nothing but the stars for company, but I always have to steel myself for that part of an overnight trip when I have to crawl into my poky canvas hideaway and try to sleep. It's something I do in order to be outdoors and in the hills, but it's not something I get a thrill out of. Obviously, part of this wariness of camping comes down to my issues with incontinence, but it's also that I just like being comfy and warm. Occasionally I even worry if that makes me a bit soft, a little less tough than those super-hikers whose books I've read and then wanted to emulate. It's probably partly why I then try and overcompensate by making things even harder than they need to be, actively avoiding comfort and doing crazy things that are physically beyond me.

Anyway, you might be wondering why I'm telling you all this, especially in a book about a long-distance hike and after already walking almost 160 kilometres in 8 days with over 9000 metres of ascending. The reason is simple. I really want to convey how blissfully, fantastically, explosively happy I was to wake up in the same bed that I would be going to sleep in later that day. I could have bounced around like Tigger at the simple prospect of having 24 more hours of guaranteed comfort ahead of me and, better still, it was raining heavily outside. Had we timed this rest day to perfection or what?

After dragging ourselves away from the delicious comfort of the mattress and dressing in our almost dry, hand-washed hiking clothes, we then ventured downstairs to the equally homely dining room where we enjoyed a very sociable breakfast with two French couples who were also staying at Gite Adalbert for the same two nights that we were. Esther practised her French over our bowls of peaches, apples and bananas and their plates of croissants, cheese and jam, while I did my best to smile and nod in all the right places. It's not that I don't speak any French at all. I can string a few basic sentences together and can usually make myself understood with a few choice hand signals. I can also, usually, make out what someone is trying to tell me if they speak slowly. However, when there are multiple conversations flying across a busy breakfast table, I might as well be trying to understand a flock of geese. Not that I minded zoning out a little. I was happy to sit back and focus on appreciating having the luxuries of life, such as a chair, a table, plates and three different pieces of cutlery instead of a spork.

Alongside Fan-fan and our fellow guests, the only other residents were Fan-fan's friendly cats lounging around the furniture. It was clear that this wasn't some investment property purchased with the intention to let rooms, but it was Fan-fan's home which she had adapted to receive guests and it was our privilege to be invited in. For such a beautiful, spotlessly clean, well-appointed and homely place it was also very reasonably priced. What we needed really had been placed right on our path at the perfect moment.

Yet as physically restful as this day would ultimately prove to be, we weren't entirely idle. This was not a day solely for lounging around even though the untrained eye may have thought so. We washed ourselves. I actually washed myself twice, taking a bath and a shower, just to make sure I got all the muck. We gave each other a much-needed back massage. We also did some catching up with our walk diary. Keeping a brief, written record of where we went, who we met and other assorted trivia was something we had done on each of our early Interrail adventures years before. At the time it had sometimes felt like such a chore, but looking back at our travel diaries more than a decade later it was invariably the apparently irrelevant details we'd decided to include, like how much the cornflakes cost, that made us smile the most. These were the kind of things we'd never have remembered otherwise and that said far more about who we were at the time than the places and museums we stumbled into.

We also found time to re-visit some of the self-care routines that had stopped abruptly the moment we had left the UK. We did a short meditation and then even took time to stretch. I always did a lot of sport as a child and so was always told about stretching and that it was apparently important. I even did quite a lot of it as part of routine warm-ups, but it's only since I've turned thirty that I've really begun to respect and appreciate the necessity of a dedicated stretch once in a while, and preferably more often. It was a fact that was really hammered home to me during the very first exercise in my very first, initially reluctant, visit to a Pilates class.

The petite, blonde, limber instructor stood at the front of the room (why hadn't I come here before again?) and began to speak, "OK, feet shoulder width apart, stand tall, shoulders up and back, now slowly roll your neck forward....good....and continue to bend forward, feel the movement one vertebrae at a time, move slowly or unfold gently back up if it gets too tight.....". All around me were geriatric ladies with their foreheads lowering towards the floor and I'd just about managed to dip my chin towards my chest before agonising spasms racked my spine. Ever since I've tried to remember to stretch more often, but usually fail unless Esther reminds me. Anyway, after 8 days of hiking it took me about ten painful minutes, edging closer and closer one millimetre at a time, before my toes even recognised my fingertips. By the way, for anyone reading this who scoffed at my mention of Pilates, I dare you to try it. And Yoga too if you think you're so tough. I'm also totally awesome at Zumba by the way, but that's another story.

After such a busy morning we decided to take a more peaceful afternoon and just lie on the bed listening to an audio book together, another pastime we had grown to especially enjoy during our time living in a motorhome. Now, having already mentioned Yoga, Pilates and the fact I don't especially look forward to sleeping in a tent in this chapter, I feel my image as a rugged tough guy may already have suffered a little. I can only imagine what is going to happen when I say that our audiobook of choice on this particular day was "When Mars and Venus Collide" by John Gray, author of the bestselling "Men Are From Mars, Women Are From Venus", so I feel I should probably explain.

After being a couple for the best part of 15 years by this point, Esther and I had been through our share of rough patches. We'd gotten together while still teenagers at university and so had basically, in large part, grown up together. This isn't a relationship book so I'm not going to go into any more details, except to say that we'd eventually learned that a relationship does take work. Not that we were going through a tough time during this hike, quite the opposite, but there is a big difference between going on an adventure like this one with a life partner compared to a group of mates. There's a lot more emotional baggage for a start, hovering just out sight but which can, in a fraction of a second, be pulled into even the most minor disagreement, a bit like pouring petrol onto a fire. Learning how to communicate better and appreciate each other, in that sense, is a bit like going on a fire safety course.

We'd only discovered John Gray's work, which revolves around the different effects that stress has on men and women and how they can better communicate and avoid conflict, completely by chance as part of a larger interview series we'd been listening to. Normally we would have dismissed such a 'popular' author as a peddler of pseudo-psychobabble, designed to shift volume and make dollars, but after just a few minutes we'd both been startled and captivated. "Do you really think like that" we had asked each other in amazement. After over a decade together it was like we could finally understand each other's language.

Anyway, out here on our hiking adventure, it just seemed very fitting to listen to another one of his books. We may not have been in an office or work environment, but we were finding the physical stress of the walk and the mental stress of making decisions and staying safe in the wild had been having a similar cumulative effect. We'd already had several, albeit productive arguments in the first week along with plenty of other teeth-clenching moments as a result of what should have been trivial occurrences but which had been heightened by physical and emotional tiredness. Making time, on this rest day, to listen to John Gray's work outlining different hormonal and emotional traits we each have (as male and female) and better understanding each other's ways of coping with them helped us diffuse any residual tension and reconnect a lot, which is hard to do when you're spending so much time walking up and down hills in single file.

All in all, we felt a lot more human going to sleep for the second time in the same, spacious, comfortable bed that we had woken up in. There was also apprehension that we would have to leave the safety of that big double bed when we woke up, but excitement as well because, somewhere along the way during our busy rest day, we had also made a big decision. Tomorrow was going to be our last day on the GR5.

Vital Statistics - Day 9
Start: Tresse
End: Tresse
Distance Hiked: Maybe 100 metres
Hiking Time: Ha ha ha
Height Gain: Up the stairs
Height Loss: Down the stairs

12. Turning Left

Our decision to part company with the GR5 did not mean that we had decided to abandon the whole adventure, we'd just decided to go a different way. We'd always known that hiking all the way to Nice in time to get back to Geneva for our flight was a long shot, but caught up in the thrill of the chase and the busyness of life on the trail we'd just ploughed on. It was only during our rest day that we'd taken the time to have a closer look at the numbers and make a more reasoned assessment. This is what we'd discovered.

According to Paddy, the route we'd completed so far should have taken us 7 days at 7 hours hiking per day, an average distance of 22 kilometres and an average vertical ascent of 1250 metres. This had actually taken us 8 days, or 9 if you count our much-needed rest day. Looking ahead, if we still wanted to make it all the way to Nice with the time we had left we'd have to average 8-hour days, cover 26 kilometres on each and still tackle 1250 metres of ascending. That was assuming we took the fastest route with no delays and no more rest days. In short, we'd have to speed up.

We'd always known that we were short on time but working it out so clinically made it all the more off-putting, especially bearing in mind how we'd been feeling after our first 8 days on the trail. Even I had to admit that it would be very hard to go faster, without a break, for more than twice as long. We didn't want to arrive in Egypt for our 'trip-of-a-lifetime' as broken physical wrecks, did we? But if we did leave the GR5, then what were we going to do instead?

On one level we had the whole of the Alps on our doorstep, we could go anywhere. But we still needed a plan, a goal, somewhere to aim at, something to get us up in the morning. As we'd come to accept on our motorhome travels, when we'd had the whole of Europe open to us, we still enjoyed ourselves more with at least a basic itinerary.

Commitment to something, anything, was what separated pleasurable travelling from aimless drifting, which is what it would have felt like to "just stay on the GR5 and see how far we get". There would be no definite, achievable goal. Plus, no matter where we got to, it would always feel somewhat unfinished.

Having a definite objective, we've found, also removes the energy-sapping leech of indecision and doubt, especially when the going gets tough. Plans can always be changed, as we were about to do with our GR5 intentions, but waking up every day not knowing 'where next' wasn't a situation we wanted to put ourselves in. We'd had spells like that in the motorhome and so much time got wasted discussing options. But what exactly were we going to do if we couldn't reach Nice?

You might be thinking at this point "it's obvious what you should do" and perhaps you're right. You might even be shouting at the page, "it says Turn Left At Mont Blanc in the bloody title, you prat". Again, you're right. However, Esther and I aren't very good at obvious solutions. Usually I put this down to our very different, almost opposite, ways of making decisions. I prefer the approach I like to call "I'll take that one please". I just like to make a decision and move on and I'm prepared to live with it even if it later turns out it wasn't the best choice, which is often. Esther, in contrast, likes to identify and then weigh up every possible option, no matter how apparently impractical. She comes up with options that wouldn't occur to me in a thousand years, such as "well, how about we take a bus to Estonia and then fly to Madrid and trek back to Barcelona before hitch-hiking to Geneva...it could work." Well, not quite to that extent, but you get the idea. When Esther makes decisions they almost always turn out to be the most advantageous choice, it just takes a lot longer to get there.

The offspring of these two opposing approaches to decision making is something we call 'leaking'. We'll be in the middle of something else, unrelated to planning, and then one of us (usually Esther) will have a brainwave and exclaim "how far would it be if we went down to Modane and then half way round the Vanoise.....". We'll then slip into a frenzied discussion before I shut it down by saying something like "OK, OK, let's just do that" and steer us back to what we had been doing in the first place, until somebody leaks again. Eventually, when we've changed our mind at least a dozen times, we sit down and slowly eliminate the various options until we settle on the least crazy. We might then still do something else.

As methods for making decisions go I should probably add that this is not an approach we'd recommend. It's inefficient, over-complicating, time-consuming and frustrating, with a tendency to turn even the most trivial decisions into unnecessarily drawn out affairs. Nowadays, we much prefer to independently clear our minds and get a feel for what we'd each like to do, sitting quietly to get in touch with our individual gut instincts, and only then come together to compare and compromise if necessary. Unfortunately, at the time of our hike, we didn't do that. Instead our decision-making process was like a reflection of our overall approach to our adventure, particularly that we were always trying to keep too many options open just in case something better came up.

Anyway, so that I don't bore you senseless with the countless variations, combinations and wacky travel plans that leaked out of us that day, I'm going to skip straight to the point. What we were going to do was take advantage of several places where major trails overlapped to create our own little custom tour. First, instead of continuing south on the GR5, for the next 5 or 6 days we would keep turning left and stay on the anti-clockwise Tour du Mont Blanc. Then, about two thirds of the way around the loop, after leaving France and passing through the Italian section, we would reach the village of Champex in Switzerland. Once we got there we would turn right, leaving the TMB and picking up the Walkers Haute Route, another well-known high-altitude trail that runs from Chamonix to Zermatt. Simple really.

This wasn't all completely plucked out of the air either. Before ultimately committing to this mish-mash of routes we did download the relevant guidebooks to make sure that it made at least some sense. The "Tour Of Mont Blanc" and "Chamonix To Zermatt", both excellently written books by Kev Reynolds and published by Cicerone Guides, contain lots of detailed route information, but what mattered most to us at the time was that the numbers checked out. If we went for it, would we have time? To our relief, the short answer was yes.

The long answer was that the portion of the TMB we planned to walk would involve 6 stages, averaging just 5 hours, 16 kilometres and 825 metres of ascending, while the portion of the Haute Route we intended to complete involved 11 stages averaging only 5 ½ hours, 13 ½ kilometres and 850 metres of ascending. That added up to 17 days of much less demanding hiking than we had been doing on the GR5, and we even had time for another rest day. It couldn't have worked out better really.

It immediately gave us a target again, helped to rid us of doubts and indecision and so lifted our spirits. We had a new objective, and what an objective it was, to mesh together portions of three of Europe's most spectacular long-distance trails. After feeling slightly disillusioned and defeated to pull out of our GR5 dash, this new plan felt even more exciting, especially since we'd spend longer at higher altitudes and amid the glacier-topped 4000 metre peaks in Switzerland. We had gone to bed at the end of our rest day with snow-capped dreams.

After another sociable, goose chatter, all-we-could-eat fruit fiesta at Gite Adalbert, and a friendly hug and farewell from our lovely host Fan-fan, we re-joined the trail. The only difference was that we didn't think of it as the GR5 anymore because we were now hiking our own unique combination. It was still a bit of a wrench to say goodbye to creature comforts, especially the bathtub, and I could hear a small part of me whispering "why not ask about a third night", but I just had to tell that part of me to stop being a wuss. The sun was shining and the rest of me was excited to be off to Zermatt, albeit by a somewhat circuitous route.

The initial going from Tresse was very easy and in less than an hour we reached Les Contamines to officially complete 'stage 1' from the Tour Of Mont Blanc guidebook, our new reference point.

I have to say, when it came to reading this new guidebook, we noticed a big shift in our attitude now that we had changed our plans. Before our rest day, whenever we had opened the GR5 guidebook and looked at the timings and place names it had felt like the book was saying "your mission, should you choose to accept it, is to get here before dark....GO!" In contrast, what the TMB guidebook seemed to be saying to us was "you could stop here, or you can carry on to here, or here....whatever suits you best, and don't forget to take a rest along the way and enjoy yourselves". Maybe this was partly down to the different writing styles of the different authors and the fact that the GR5 stages actually were more demanding with far fewer places to stay, on average, but I reckon it was mostly a complete change in our own mindset. We were no longer stressed about not making it in time because we now felt we had a realistic objective.

Our apparently newfound willingness to only cover sensible distances that suited out bodies was further confirmed by our immediate decision not to try and complete the whole of the suggested TMB 'stage 2' by the end of the day either, a stage that just happened to be the most demanding of the entire guidebook itinerary. Even though it 'only' involved 7 hours of hiking over 18 kilometres with 1316 metres ascent and 929 metres of descent, much less than we had covered on several of our GR5 days, we saw no reason to use up all of our renewed energy right away, not with time in hand. Instead we elected to do the uphill part but then stay high, camping after around 5 hours somewhere close to the Refuge de la Croix Bonhomme at 2426 metres altitude.

Apart from a few boding clouds on the southern horizon, in the direction we were heading, the weather was now very warm and we felt very at home in Les Contamines. Two years earlier we had visited the village in Homer, our motorhome, and had enjoyed several lovely day hikes on the surrounding hills, one of which happened to include most of the route that we would be walking for the rest of the day. Feeling like we knew what lay ahead for a change made us feel even more relaxed. Sure, we remembered the path ahead of us being steep and busy with people, but since the weather was so fine why not sit back and enjoy a long, leisurely and rather large lunch of fresh fruit before heading upwards.

You could say we were struggling to get going again after such a relaxed time at Gite Adalbert, which was true, but it didn't diminish the pleasure of our melon, frozen berries, fresh figs, chestnuts and soy yoghurt feast one bit. We ate this tasty bounty sitting in the shade by the picturesque chapel of Notre Dame de la Gorge while listening to another few chapters of our John Gray audiobook. It just seemed a far more sensible and pleasant way to pass the early afternoon instead of hiking in the heat of the day, or the cool of the evening come to that. Maybe heading back to Fan-fan's wasn't such a bad idea after all?

We eventually set off for the almost 1400m climb ahead of us just after 3 p.m. and were pleasantly surprised at just how good we felt. Our bellies were bloated and our bags were easily as heavy as they had been when we'd set out from Lac Leman, probably heavier with all of the dry food we still had with us from Les Houches plus some cucumbers and tomatoes from Les Contamines, but with a week of hiking to condition ourselves combined with our rest day we couldn't help wondering where the fearsome gradients we remembered from two years earlier had gone.

93

The opening portion of the climb was relatively steep and rocky but soon levelled out after 250 metres of ascent to pass the Refuge Nant Borrant, already busy with evening and overnight guests lounging on the terrace. After another hour or so of gentle climbing, along a wide gravel track with green fields and trees on both sides, we passed the soothingly named Refuge de la Balme at 1706 metres. From here the path kicked up sharply again and turned stonier underfoot. We were about to re-enter the world of the high mountains above 2000 metres and were enjoying the sheer exposed rock faces, scree slopes and waterfalls that came with it. The sound of chirruping marmots was also in the air so we passed the time playing 'spot the marmot', with each of us notching up a couple of fluffy sightings.

Reaching the Col du Bonhomme at 2329 metres we quickly ducked into the wooden shelter, which looks a little like a very high-altitude bus stop, to put on our hats and gloves and most of our other base layers to guard against the rapidly gathering chill. At this altitude there were plenty of dirty snow patches still resisting the summer sun, and with a low cloud blowing in fast from the higher rocky parts of the mountain it had suddenly become decidedly nippy. In the space of just a few minutes we had apparently passed from summer to winter hiking. Despite the cold we still munched our way happily through the 500 grams of organic vine tomatoes I'd been carrying uphill for the last 1200 metres, now that the melon, berries, figs and chestnuts seemed to have made a little space.

The final section of hiking required to reach our planned overnight pitch at the Refuge de la Croix du Bonhomme was relatively short, but was still hard work across an often uneven traverse. The views to the south were incredible, reaching down into the deep green valleys below us and across the summits level with our eyeline. Around three quarters of an hour later we passed over the high point for the day, the Col de la Croix du Bonhomme at

2483 metres. At this altitude the clouds were whipping quickly right over our heads, so close we could almost touch them by standing on our tip-toes. Beautiful, but also filthily cold, so we didn't pause too long to revel in our accomplishment at ascending almost 1400 metres since Les Contamines. Just 5 minutes away and 50 metres below us was the place we planned to rest our heads for the night.

We arrived at the Refuge de la Croix du Bonhomme just before 7 p.m. I confess I was feeling a little daunted at the prospect of staying 'at' a refuge, even though we would be outside in our tent. Despite many years of hiking, including numerous wild camping experiences in the Lake District, this was going to be our first ever experience up close and personal with a high mountain refuge at night. We'd stayed at youth hostels in the Lake District and we'd sat outside of high mountain huts on day walks, but had never actually taken the step of going inside, except very rarely to use a toilet. I'm not really sure why. Partly, I suppose, the need just hadn't arisen. Then there were my issues around crowds and confined spaces stemming from my childhood experiences of incontinence. And I suppose I always rather liked the solitude of hiking in the wilderness and was worried that having to make small talk or, knowing me, competitive banter with other hikers would detract from the experience somewhat. I still don't know why I was quite so nervous though. Images of cowboys swaggering into smoky saloons, with all eyes swivelling to stare at them as they stood on the threshold, came to mind as I prepared to go in.

I needn't have worried of course. All of the many and varied hikers inside were far more wrapped up in their own food and company to pay us any attention. We were just one of dozens of strangers passing in and out of the warmth every minute, exchanging muddy boots for the refuge-provided footwear on the way. The dining room was literally full to capacity with overnight guests, munching on what looked to be the practically mandatory pasta and cheese based concoction. Moisture hung in the air and condensed silently on the windows of the hut. It was half dining room, half steam room, where the smell of dinner fought for supremacy over the smell of effort and well-worn socks.

The building itself was a wooden construction and looked like it had stood the test of many tough winters. As we would discover later, while trying to find a toilet, the sleeping chambers and facilities upstairs had the feel of a rabbit warren. Low lighting created an atmosphere of quiet, which I guess was the idea, with darkened corridors busy with soft-footed guests, each visible for just a short distance before vanishing around a corner. Upstairs it was calm, or at least as calm as possible with hundreds of strangers wedging their gear into corners and preparing to snore, or lie awake, alongside each other in vast halls of bunk beds. Downstairs it was a feeding frenzy.

We found one of the hut guardians, members of staff who live at the hut for long periods and prepare meals, do DIY, cleaning etc., and they immediately confirmed it was fine for us to camp nearby, for free, and still use the facilities if we wished. Not only was this a big relief for us, but it also seemed like a kind and generous gesture that was in keeping with the spirit of mountain refuges. Despite my long-held reservations about getting too close to mountain refuges, we had still done research in the past regarding their prices and their policies on camping nearby etc., just in case. However, all we'd really been able to learn was that refuge websites tended to be either ambiguous on the subject of allowing people to stay outside, or declared an outright policy of not tolerating it. Therefore, although we'd basically been planning to camp somewhere near the Refuge de la Croix du Bonhomme all day, until we actually asked we didn't know whether it would be officially allowed or not. Being allowed to use the facilities as well was an entirely unexpected bonus.

Not that we would be entirely freeloading by doing so I should probably add, because, two days prior to leaving the UK and for the sum total of around £70, we had each signed up as members of the UK branch of the Austrian Alpine Club. Not only did this mean that we each had additional rescue insurance in the high mountains but it also meant that part of our membership fee went towards supporting the many centrally owned and managed refuges throughout the Alps through something called "the reciprocal agreement". And, since the Refuge de la Croix du Bonhomme was owned and operated by the Club Alpin Francaise (CAF), that meant that we had contributed at least a very small amount towards our night of facilities. Given the amazing service and peace of mind that refuges provide to hikers, not just in summer but also in winter when they often make winter bunks available, contributing to their upkeep even in this small way seemed like the least we could do, no matter how little use we originally intended to make of them.

Since the dining room was so busy and there was a queue for the few gas rings in the guest kitchen, we went back outside to the chilly terrace to fire up our own burner and prepare dinner. We had buckwheat pasta with an avocado, cucumber, shallot, fresh garlic, stem ginger and turmeric root salsa. Well, I say salsa. It would have been more of a salsa if we hadn't eaten most of our tomatoes an hour earlier at the Col du Bonhomme, or bothered to actually chop and mix the ingredients together instead of just eating them one at a time, but it still tasted bloody good. Our rather different, veggie-based style of alfresco dining caught the attention of a few other refuge visitors who had just been enjoying the cheese-fest inside. It was actually quite nice to explain how we try and maintain our food choices, as much as we can, to support our bodies on such a challenging trek while also sticking to our principles. The people seemed genuinely interested and listened intently, which made me feel slightly less daft for having carried over a kilo of salad food uphill for the past 5 hours. I'd only been there half an hour and I was already starting to feel quite at home.

Oh, and I nearly forgot to mention, but the view from the Refuge de la Croix du Bonhomme is simply awesome. Sitting on a shoulder of the Mont Blanc massif, at almost 2500 metres, it would be hard for it not to be. Hills and pointed peaks are almost uncountable and they seem to jostle for space on the horizon. It may well be the most beautiful place in Europe to sit outside on a freezing cold picnic bench and eat cold salad food while your meth's burner fights a losing battle against the weather to get some water boiling. Possibly.

As the sun began to set most of the other guests began vanishing into the fuggy depths of the refuge to find their bunks, and we went into the night to pitch our tent. There were at least a dozen other tents in the area we'd been asked to camp in, making finding a flat spot that wasn't already occupied a little tricky in the dark, but soon enough we had done the necessary erecting, inflating and unfolding. We then decided to make the most of the nearby refuge and went back to sit in the warm for a little longer, review the route for the morning and enjoy our first experience of a mountain refuge after dark, with people playing cards, laughing and joking. Another first for us, and a pleasant one. Nothing was boisterous, nothing was loud, it was just tranquil, communal happiness.

Eventually we could linger no longer and so, wrapping ourselves in fluffy jackets and gloves, we made the jarring transition from light and warmth to darkness and a cold so intense it took our breath away. We hastened, as fast as was safe, to the door of our squat little tent and found it looking vulnerable and insignificant against the silhouettes of gigantic mountains now visible against stars. It was hard to believe that we were really going to sleep out here, in this vast wilderness, with nothing but a few paper-thin layers of fabric between us and this monumental void. I don't think that we had ever seen the Milky Way Galaxy quite so vividly as we saw it that night. Were it not for the biting cold starting to gnaw away the indoor warmth that we'd trapped within our layers, I think we might have stood there transfixed until morning.

Vital Statistics - Day 10
Start: Tresse
End: Refuge de la Croix du Bonhomme
Distance Hiked: 16 kilometres
Hiking Time: 6 hours
Height Gain: 1400 metres
Height Loss: 150 metres

13. Know Your Limits

Gritting our teeth against the bitterly cold air that was freezing our lips and nostrils, we struggled out of our sleeping bags, contorted ourselves into our moist and crumpled hiking clothes, and emerged into the new day. It was 7 a.m. and at over 2400 metres this was a sunrise to treasure. Shivering in the shade alongside our frosty tent, we watched the light silently chase the shadows away from mountain peaks and push them further and further into the valleys below.

It had not exactly been a restful night. Our sleeping bags were rated "comfortable" down to freezing temperature, but judging by the frozen condensation all over our tent the overnight chill had dipped a little further than that. Still, waking to a sight like this was a great way to erase memories of the sleepless hours. Fellow campers were also emerging around us, nodding and smiling, before swiftly packing their gear and wandering off in their chosen direction. We were simply content to absorb the view, hold hands and romantically synchronise our chattering teeth.

This morning was a watershed in our adventure. It was the moment at which we would officially part company with the GR5. After almost ten full days living and hiking along its length, the GR5 was about to continue south-east, whereas we would remain on the TMB and swing left around Europe's highest mountain.

Our immediate destination after leaving the refuge was technically a variant of the 'standard' TMB route. That there are so many waymarked variants is one of the best features of the TMB, and it helps a lot that Kev Reynolds has done such a great job of laying out the combinations intuitively in his guidebook, allowing hikers to almost effortlessly create a route suited to their own preferences.

The variant we had chosen to follow would involve climbing a little further from the refuge in order to cross the

2665 metre Col des Fours, instead of heading immediately downhill into the hamlet of Les Chapieux. Along with another possible variant on a later stage, this was the highest point reached on the entire TMB and the reason we wanted to go that way was simple. The weather was great and we were already at 2443 metres. With just another 200 metres of ascending required it seemed like a lot of reward for apparently minimal effort.

Also, as an added bonus, it hadn't escaped our notice that by going that way we would be cutting the corner on the 'standard' route by at least an hour, and possibly even 2 hours if we made good time. "So what?" you may ask, "I thought you'd both agreed to take it easy and only do sensible stages from now on, following your new plan. Why do you care about shaving off an hour or two?" Well, I have to admit, that's a very good question, so I'd better try and explain.

The reason we had 'temporarily' decided to care about going faster was because, while we had been warming ourselves the previous evening in the cosy refuge, we had also been looking at the route ahead and the various accommodation options on offer along the way. One of the things we'd noticed was that there was apparently nowhere to camp in the town of Courmayeur, but that it was explicitly suggested as being a good place for a rest day. "What a great idea" we'd thought. "If that's the next place we're going to have to fork out for a room anyway, why don't we have our next rest day there as well? We had such a great time at Fan-fan's. It's perfect. And hey, since we're shaving an hour or two off the standard route by taking the Col des Fours variant, then it's 'only' ten hours hiking or so all the way from here to Courmayeur. I bet we can do it in a day, especially if know we have a rest day immediately afterwards. It'll even make it an 'extra' rest day, because we'll have saved an entire day. We've already done some 9-hour days so it's not that much further and I bet we'll feel great afterwards."

101

Now I expect you're probably dazzled at this point by the overwhelming genius of our audacious plan. All we had to do to 'buy' ourselves another whole day of complete, unmitigated rest was to walk for an extra hour or two. Simple, but brilliant. It would be like putting a pound in the bank on Monday and finding it had turned into ten pounds by Wednesday. What faultless logic. When you put it like that, what could possibly go wrong?

You may also be thinking that, with such a particularly long day of hiking in mind, we would have hastened away towards the Col des Fours shortly after sunrise, but we didn't. Evidently rapid starts were still not our forte. By the time we had stuffed away our sleeping kit, rolled up our sodden tent, made use of the toilets and chewed our way through a breakfast of our remaining tomatoes and cucumber on the terrace of the refuge, it appeared that all of the other overnight guests had vanished into thin air. They'd been there when we sat down to eat, milling around all over the place, filling up water bottles, adjusting straps and lacing up their boots, but now they'd all apparently gone. "Oh well" I thought, "we'll just have to overtake them later".

The only creatures that did hang around to see us off were a large family of ibex who calmly emerged from behind the crest of a ridge just as we set out, and then paused to chew the cud while their young calves played around them. Positioned as they were, magnificently framed against the brilliant blue sky and rock faces on the horizon, it was like a wildlife photographers fantasy moment and all we'd done to deserve it was to give our breakfast a bloody good chew. Obviously, it was going to be a great day.

Despite being the highest point of the TMB, the ascent to the Col des Fours from the refuge was actually very gradual and easy, only slightly hampered by an extensive patch of slushy snow and ice immediately before the col. Unfortunately, due to some clouds hanging around on the very top of Mont Blanc, the "shining dome of snow

102

and ice" described in the guidebook wasn't visible to us, but it hardly diminished the abundant, awesome scenery we could still see.

Gazing into the far distance we could make out saw-like, jagged summits decorated with snow patches as far as the haze would allow. Looking a little closer, but still far below us, we could make out the various pathways that snaked along the Vallée des Glaciers between Les Chapieux and the Col de la Seigne, where France turned into Italy. Closer still, on the slopes all around us, were boulders and scree of all shapes and sizes that served as a reminder of how even these enormous mountains wouldn't last forever, broken down over the millennia by the gradual but incessant cycle of hot and cold. Then, much, much closer, between the soles of our feet we found several incredible fossil impressions of sea creatures embedded in the fabric of the Alps, a relic of former aeons when even the ground beneath our feet was beneath the waves somewhere or other. It was a very special moment, reflecting on the complex and awesome timescales of nature compared to our own fleeting existence.

The descent from the Col des Fours into the Vallée des Glaciers proved to be much more technical and challenging than we had expected, with lots of snow patches, loose shale and gigantic boulders to negotiate but with no single, clearly defined route that we could see to get us started. In the end we just picked our way carefully in the direction gravity wanted us to go, roughly pointing ourselves in the direction our map and compass suggested was correct and hoping that we'd come across a more definite trail, which we eventually did. The steepness of the descent also began to ease as the scree and slush gave way to mud and sludge, one result of which was an astonishingly high-speed face plant suffered by another nearby hiker. The young girl in question, understandably, didn't seem too pleased with her unexpected plunge, but the rest of her family found the whole event hilarious, as did I, although I didn't laugh quite as loudly as her parents. Now that's the stuff family holidays are made of.

Two and a half hours after setting out, having lost almost 900 metres in altitude since the Col des Fours, we crossed the river flowing down the Vallée des Glaciers and fortified ourselves with a brief stop to eat dried apricots. Immediately ahead of us was another 700 metres of uphill hiking to reach the French-Italian border at the Col de la Seigne (2516 metres), a broad and flat gap in an otherwise steep and rocky ridgeline.

Heading up towards the Col de la Seigne was easy at first but steepened towards the top. It was a very pretty climb with wild flowers flickering in the wind, marmots dashing noisily from burrow to burrow and plenty of other hikers to say "Bonjour", or occasionally "Buongiorno", to as well. There was a definite friendly and supportive atmosphere in the air. We even saw one gentleman giving a companion a piggy-back up the final few hundred metres of ascending, with both his own and his friend's rucksack slung across his front. It was an impressive feat of both strength and friendship to observe as we reached the edge of France.

It's at times like this, on busy trails, that Esther and I like to try and collect as many smiles as we can from passing hikers. I think it was the famous Alfred Wainwright, author of the very special pictorial guides to the Lake District, who was asked once about saying hello to passing hikers and responded by saying that it wasn't compulsory. That he could always head off in another direction or hide. I get that, I really do. There are some days when the last thing I want to be doing is saying 'hello' every 15 seconds as the passing hordes merge into a near monotonous blur of bright colours and the scent of suncream. But I still always try and remind myself to smile and say hello anyway as they pass. There are many beautiful sights in the mountains and I think that a warm smile should be one of them. I'd rather people passed me

104

thinking "what was that idiot grinning at?" instead of "what a miserable bastard". Never underestimate the power of a smile.

Views from the Col de la Seigne surpassed even those earlier in the day from the Col des Fours, despite Mont Blanc still being hidden by the weather. Looking south, back into France and along the Vallée des Glaciers that we had just climbed, was a stunning view of snowy peaks framed by steep-sided valley walls and crags. Looking north, into Italy, was an equally magnificent if very different view with a deep and bare trench of a valley vanishing away beneath the cloudy hills. The exotic names of various rock spires and ice flows, that should have been on display, tantalised us from the pages of the guidebook but it just wasn't to be this time. Still, the Col de la Seigne had a definite, powerful, attractive force that made it tempting to just sit and watch the afternoon pass by. Or maybe we were just getting tired?

After another (brief) snack of ryebread and two dried apricots each, all we had left that didn't need cooking, it was time to start the long descent into Italy. There were plenty of trails to choose from, with probably half a dozen apparent tracks on the ground, although the guidebook assured us they would all soon reunite. They did. Just ten minutes later and we found ourselves stopping again at the old customs house of La Casermetta (2356 metres) which had been converted into a museum by the Espace Mont-Blanc project.

Normally a free museum like this, in a city centre perhaps, would have been just the kind of place we would have spent time browsing. Today, however, in anticipation of the hours and hours of walking still ahead of us it was hardly ideal. Yet the displays inside proved to be so compelling and informative that half an hour vanished almost before we knew it. Of particular interest, alongside the flora and fauna displays, was the large relief map of the Mont Blanc massif that allowed us to appreciate, for the first time, the scale and variation of the undertaking we had stumbled somewhat accidentally into. Tracing out the many ups and downs of the TMB in green and grey papier maché may have been a far cry, physically, from the real thing but mentally it gave us much more clarity about what was to come.

Another hour of hiking later and the Rifugio Elisabetta appeared, perched on a rocky spur set against the backdrop of an enormous, tumbling glacier called the Glacier de la Lée Blanche. Ever since leaving the Col de la Seigne we had been enjoying the flowing, rocky scenery, but this first glimpse of a glacier so close to the trail made us stop in our tracks. Glaciers are so enormous and powerful and yet also so apparently vulnerable, diminishing year on year, that we always find them thoughtful and moving sights. Pausing to imagine the carved and bare hillside beyond the tongue of ice as it would have looked just decades earlier can also be quite a melancholy moment, and so it proved here also. This was a place that could easily appear almost untouched by modern civilisation, with only an occasional building or man-made signpost on display, and yet it was still changing faster than ever before as a result of human action.

Tearing ourselves away, yet another hour of walking along a flat and green plain followed, the ground criss-crossed with thin rivulets of water feeding the peaceful Lac Combal. To our left and right the valley walls rose steeply while directly ahead a gigantic tree-covered moraine seemed to be blocking our path. This was the moraine left behind by the Glacier de Miage, whose high-altitude starting point we could only just make out, appearing just above the rubble ridge as a thin sliver of white emerging from the snow-covered mountain tops.

It was at around this point, approaching 5 p.m. and surrounded by pristine mountain scenery, that we quite unexpectedly found ourselves staring defeat in the face. Like a marathon runner hitting the wall at mile twenty, as much as we had wanted and anticipated continuing to follow the standard TMB for another 4 ½ hours, over the Mont Favre spur and all the way down to Courmayeur before stopping, our energy levels had suddenly taken a dive. Well, I say suddenly, they'd probably been dwindling for quite a while but we'd only just taken the time to notice. It was only when the guidebook pointed out that it was possible to take a short detour up the moraine, to appreciate the full and imposing sight of the Glacier de Miage, that we realised quite how knackered we were. Normally we would have jumped at the chance to have a good view of a glacier, but this time we couldn't face it. More than anything we just wanted to curl up in a ball and go to sleep.

I was also confused. I mean, we'd only been walking for 7 hours so far and we'd done longer days than that during the previous week without feeling quite so bad. What was it that we'd failed to take account of? And then it struck me. We may have been walking for 'only' 7 hours, but we'd already covered 22 kilometres with 1000 metres of climbing and 1600 metres of descending in that time, numbers which were more than comparable with our longest days on the GR5. The previous evening we'd only been adding up the timings, but we hadn't factored in the distances and altitude changes. What we'd felt was achievable when described simply as a 10-hour day, was actually a 36-kilometre epic with 1500 metres of ascent and 2700 metres of descent.

We also hadn't factored in any leeway for slowing down as we grew tired, which is exactly what we had been doing ever since the Col de la Seigne. What we'd budgeted 5 ½ hours for had taken us 7, and there was still 4 ½ - 5 hours to go. If we did try and 'finish it' we were looking at a 12-hour day that ended after dark.

"Shit" I thought, "we've only gone and done it again". Like moths to a flame, through a combination of arrogance, impatience and a failure to plan in enough detail, we'd bitten off far more than we could chew only a day after resolving to be more sensible.

It was lucky really that we'd crashed and burned right where there was still a viable 'escape route', a variant listed in the guidebook as the "bad-weather option". Basically, instead of going up and over the big rocky lump to our right in order to reach Courmayeur in 4 ½ - 5 hours, we could go straight downhill into the Val Veni and loop around the end of the rocky lump instead. According to our guidebook this would save a whole hour of hiking and, if we needed them (which we almost certainly would), there were a couple of campsites along the way. As much as we were disappointed not to see the "full sweeping majesty of crag, spire, snow-dome, rockface and nosing glacier" that the high route apparently provided, our spent limbs dictated that it was the low road for us.

We lost altitude quickly following a tarmac road and the temperature seemed to rise rapidly. On the one hand such speedy progress was very welcome, since it would surely bring us to a place of rest that much sooner, but on the other hand our bodies were really not appreciating this gravity driven, jarring and jolting rhythm. Each lethargic step sent a new impact up through our joints that shook our vital organs and wobbled our wobbly bits. I felt like a ragdoll that had been forced into acting like a buffer between the road and my rucksack. We soon found ourselves counting every step, every metre and every minute. Our mantra of "just keep walking" was being edged out by another, more desperate plea of "how much further can this go on for?"

After around half an hour of painful plodding we spotted a weather-beaten sign for "camping" which pointed along a small track by the side of the road and we thought our salvation was finally near at hand. By chance, a rather dapper looking Italian couple were also considering the sign as a possible short cut back to their car, which they had parked next to a campsite earlier in the day. We assembled a small, impromptu committee to check our map. It was hard to be certain exactly where on the road we all were, but based on some recent twists and turns and a handful of other visual clues, the consensus emerged that surely we must be next to "that narrow, dotted line", the one which cut more or less directly from the twisting road towards one of the camping symbols marked on the map. It looked like it was indeed a short cut. Brilliant. We didn't quite high-five each other but I think that was the prevailing mood.

So, we set off, as a four, making polite small talk that I'm sure we all fully expected would last no longer than the quarter of an hour or so it would take to reach our mutual destination. The Italian gentleman in particular, dressed in neatly ironed cream trousers, brown leather shoes and a pastel pink shirt, proved to be an interesting walking companion who spoke excellent English. Still, conversation began to falter as quarter of an hour turned into half an hour, and then three quarters of an hour, and there was still no apparent end in sight. Nobody it seemed wanted to say the obvious, that we had been wrong to follow the sign. Not only was the path now worryingly overgrown but it was also going uphill. Far, far below we could just about make out, through the trees, the sight of two adjacent campsites by the side of the road.

As one of the two supposed 'hikers' in the group I have to say I felt a particular weight of responsibility for the blunder and felt a growing urge to take action. As we drew roughly level with the distant campsites I spotted an even less obvious and more overgrown track on our left and, since it apparently went downhill, I suggested we all follow it. What came next involved ducking under tree branches, crashing through ancient brambles, getting stuck in loose and muddy soil and negotiating the debris left by a logging operation. Somewhere along the way our Italian companions began to lag behind, probably supposing their self-appointed English guide had little clue what he was doing. Or maybe they just wanted me to be the first to fall down any hidden drops.

Perseverance paid off in the end though. After what seemed like an age we emerged into a clearing directly above one of the campsites. My face was sticky with cobwebs, our hair was full of bracken and fir branches, dirt and soil was mixed with suncream and sweat, but we had made it and we were all still alive. All that remained was to pick our way down the steep, grassy bank of a ski-slope to finally reach the field of tents. I was so relieved I felt like I had won the Olympics. The day could finally end and I hadn't killed two elderly Italians by hijacking their gentle stroll and cajoling them through a jungle of trees.

Incidentally, it soon became apparent after we'd pitched our tent and gorged on the ripe melons and other fruit being sold in the campsite reception, that this would have been the second campsite we'd have reached had we stayed on the road. Whether that sign had been deliberately put up by the owners of this particular camping in order to divert trade away from their competitors, perhaps based on the assumption that at least half of their victims would survive the detour, we would never know for sure. We were just too bloody tired to ask. Lovely campsite though!

Vital Statistics - Day 11
Start: Refuge de la Croix du Bonhomme
End: Camping Val Veni
Distance Hiked: 30 kilometres
Hiking Time: 9 hours
Height Gain: 1000 metres
Height Loss: 2100 metres

14. Up And Over Anyway

Blue skies greeted us once again on this, our twelfth day since leaving the shores of Lac Leman, and the bright, already hot sun seemed to make the Alps surrounding us even more Alpine somehow. From the green of the pines on the trees, the grey of the vertical rock faces, the beige of the sun-baked ski-slopes and even the white of the snow, it all seemed just a little more vivid than normal. It felt like we had woken up on the set of the Sound of Music, except without Julie Andrews and a lot more melons. Or maybe there had just been something in the beans we'd had for dinner?

In hindsight, we probably hadn't really needed dinner the night before, not after the mountains of fresh fruit we had practically inhaled within half an hour of pitching our tent. There are only so many melons that can fit inside a human body after all, assuming you only use the conventional entry point anyway. But then Esther had also discovered a bumper bag of frozen beans in the campsite shop and we'd gotten a little overexcited. Since we had stopped eating meat, beans had become a staple of our meals at home, being high in both protein and in carbohydrates, so even though we were no longer especially hungry we decided that our depleted bodies would probably benefit from a few beans.

Two hours later and what we'd actually managed to create was a soupy, stodgy, beany mix that would have easily fed a dozen hungry builders. Supplementing the kilogram of beans we'd acquired with another kilogram of a frozen vegetable medley, we'd then scrounged a 3-litre saucepan from the campsite owner, added two tins of chopped tomatoes, a few dashes of herbs, and, hey presto, had created the dietary equivalent of a fibre-laden sledgehammer. It had taken an almost heroic effort to consume just a third of the pan before we'd finally crawled

111

into our sleeping bags clutching aching tummies. It looked like it was going to have to be beans for breakfast, lunch and dinner the next day as well.

Needless to say, the interior of our tent had also been somewhat loud and fragrant during the night. Thankfully we didn't have any neighbours too close by. More than a decade earlier, during one of our Interrail adventures, we'd pitched our tent in an almost empty campsite and gone out for the day, returning after dark to find that somebody with an enormous Harley Davidson had pitched their tent just ten centimetres away from ours and was snoring like a pneumatic drill. He hadn't even bothered to close his tent and we could see him, a large man, still fully dressed and sprawled out on his back like a leather wrapped starfish. Obviously, I was all for waking him and asking him to move his tent to somewhere else in the almost empty field, but Esther talked me out of it. In the end we slept in the toilet block. Anyway, the last thing I wanted here in Italy was someone complaining that my farting was keeping them awake. It wasn't what we'd eaten that was causing problems, it had been a wonderfully nutritious meal, we'd just eaten way, way too much.

Surprisingly, the powerful aroma we were each producing was exactly the same as when we'd experimented with making our own dehydrated meals several years earlier. It had been part of the preparation for our original GR5/honeymoon/career break attempt. We'd spent months making enormous batches of vegetable stew, ladling portions on to non-stick sheets in an electric food dehydrator, baking them at low temperature for hours on end and then sticking them in the food processor to make our own powdered soup. We'd had a real production line going and managed to make about 40 kilograms of the stuff. Yet no matter what stew we started out with, whenever we added water and boiled it up, the product tasted almost exactly the same. You could just about tell if something had started life as tomato based or curry flavoured, but that was about it. And the farts were always identical, pungent and copious. Astonishingly, we'd somehow managed to recreate them on the TMB now as well.

Tragically, while packing away our stuff in the sunshine, I accidentally sent the remaining two litres of our beany stodge flying all over the grass outside of our tent. For Esther especially, who hates wasting food with a passion, this was a devastating spill. Now, I don't want to cast aspersions on Esther's cooking skills but, unbelievably, this made it look even less appetising. I knew it was only beans and veggies. Esther knew it was only beans and veggies. But all of the other campers surrounding us surely wouldn't hesitate to conclude that one of us had stepped out of our tent in the middle of the night to throw up and/or shit on the floor. If you've never tried scooping gloopy bean mix out of long, damp grass I assure you it is not a pleasant task, especially not with well-to-do, elderly ladies muttering as they pass by and watch you handling 'dog vomit' with your bare hands.

It was half past ten by the time we'd packed up, cleaned up and eaten a back-up breakfast melon in preparation for the hiking ahead of us. Having failed to reach Courmayeur the previous day, and nearly crippling ourselves in the attempt, our main objectives now were to reach the town quickly, find a room and then rest ourselves with a quiet afternoon and a good night's sleep. In theory, this could be achieved most easily by continuing along the relatively level floor of the Val Veni and then looping around the end of the big rocky lump that still stood between us and Courmayeur, a route that would take no more than a couple of hours to complete. However, with our 'defeat' from the previous afternoon still throbbing in our legs and the feeling that we had already missed out on the views that the balcony route between Lac Combal and the Col Checrouit was supposed to offer, we decided to throw caution to the wind and go up and over the rocky lump anyway.

Scrambling back up the 'almost-certainly-not-a-real-path' route that we had pioneered with our doubtful Italian partners the previous evening, we eventually managed to find a real signpost that confirmed we were now going up the right part of the correct hill. The only slight knock to my inflated sense of direction was that a couple carrying a young child, who had started out from the camping at the same time as us but that had followed a well-manicured path in the opposite direction, were already stood at the same signpost. Apparently, my face-scratching, log jumping, cobweb dodging route was not the most direct way after all.

The temperature was rising fast with the morning sun now high in the sky, so we felt very grateful to be climbing this 400-metre ascent to the Col Checrouit (1956 metres) on the shaded side of the hill. Passing by a couple of cabins we rose quickly, with the amazing rock wall of the Aiguille Noire towering over us each time we paused to catch our breath. This 3773-metre summit had been shrouded in cloud for most of the previous day so the frequent references to it in the guidebook had been somewhat wasted on us, but not anymore. It was a truly staggering natural wonder that such a high peak could rise so vertically and, since we were pretty close to the base, we were getting the full vertigo inducing effect. It was stunning.

The descent from the col into Courmayeur took two and a half hot and stifling hours, and I frequently found myself looking jealously up at the cable car passengers gliding effortlessly to and from the col above our heads. It really was a long and dusty drag downhill and there was very little wind to temper the baking afternoon sun. Not that it was unpleasant or ugly, far from it. It may not have been the most spectacular portion of the TMB, but we were still getting to enjoy the most wonderful flurries of colourful butterflies that swarmed around us as we passed by, along

114

with sightings of salamanders, ladybirds and the most incredibly fat bees that we'd ever seen.

We reached the cobbled suburbs of Courmayeur and, based on the well-tended houses with their exposed beams, window boxes and balconies, it was fairly obvious we were passing through an affluent area, a fact that was confirmed by the prices quoted at the handful of hotels we enquired in. Our legs might have wanted us to stop asap, but our wallet continued to crack the whip all the way into the town centre where we threw ourselves upon the mercy of the tourist information office. Our back-up plan, as usual, was that if rooms proved too prohibitively expensive then we'd resupply with food and just keep walking. Of course, as plans go, ours was rubbish. We were hot, tired, sweaty and both mentally and physically in need of a rest, and yet our ego regarding rooms was still hovering in the background and using the cost as an excuse to drive us onwards. We wouldn't have hesitated to spend money on a couple of punnets of organic blueberries and a bottle of kombucha, but an extra tenner on a room made us edgy. It was like having financial bipolar disorder, elevating one aspect of our wellbeing while dismissing another, and we both knew it too.

Thankfully we didn't need our abysmal back up plan. The staff at the busy tourist office in Courmayeur proved to be both overwhelmingly friendly and well-informed. In no time at all we were sitting in our own room at Pension Venezia, a basic 1-star hotel with twin beds, a shared bathroom and even our own south facing balcony. The cost was just 43 euros. In a town cluttered with boutique stores and high-priced fashion, it was really very reasonably priced and, as an added bonus, it was pretty much directly on the TMB route.

One brief trip to the supermarket later and we were sitting down to a buffet dinner of salad leaves, borlotti beans, tomato, cucumber, courgette and tofu while overlooking the glaciated Mont Blanc Massif on our own private balcony. It really didn't matter how many stars our home for the night had, it was bloody perfection.

Later on that evening, almost as an homage to our younger days of student travel when simply walking through town centres was one of our main forms of entertainment, we headed out after sunset to explore the clean and busy streets of Courmayeur. Walking in the cool of the evening, holding hands, we couldn't help smiling at the serenity we both felt deep inside. Up in the mountains, even in the tent resting at night, I'm always aware of a residual alertness, a part of my mind that stays focused on safety and security and that never quite switches off. Well, it turns out that aimlessly and indifferently browsing shop windows, full of stuff I neither want or need, is the perfect way for me to release that tension, or at least it was on this particular evening anyway.

And besides, with our tatty flip-flops, trail-beaten feet, bruised hips and shoulders, still damp and stained hand-washed clothes, chapped lips, various vivid tan lines on display, a meal in our stomachs and a bed to go home to, what more could we have possibly needed anyway?

Vital Statistics - Day 12
Start: Camping Val Veni
End: Courmayeur
Distance Hiked: 10 kilometres
Hiking Time: 4 hours
Height Gain: 500 metres
Height Loss: 800 metres

15. Twenty In A Bed

We headed out of Courmayeur uncharacteristically early the next day, before 10 a.m., feeling refreshed and excited. The air was still and it was already pleasantly warm, with a bright blue sky that was clear of clouds and looking innocent in every way. Our guidebook promised that "in good conditions this stage promises to be one of the highlights of the Tour of Mont Blanc" and we didn't want to dither and miss the view, especially with a thunderstorm forecast by nightfall.

Not that the impending bad weather was too much of a worry because, after nearly two weeks of relying on our luck and questionable judgement to find places to sleep, for the first time ever we had made a reservation at a mountain refuge, the privately owned Rifugio Bonatti. By evening the sky could spit out as much rain, thunder and hail as it wanted, and I still wouldn't have to put a tent up in it.

Trying to book a place had been a last-minute idea, just before bed, motivated only by the terrible weather forecast. Given that it was August and the middle of the high season, I hadn't been overly optimistic about our chances of getting a space and yet it had all worked out with surprising speed. By the time we'd woken up we'd already had an email back saying that they'd reserved us 2 bunks in their dortoir. How great was that! I was genuinely touched that, with no deposit required and based on nothing more than an out of the blue email, they were willing to hold two beds for us. All they asked was that we do our best to let them know if our plans changed.

Apparently we'd come a long way, and not just physically, since leaving Thonon-les-Bains 12 days earlier. Who were these lean, trail-stained, sweat-marked and tan-lined athletes bounding into the wilderness with just the right amount of gear, just the right amount of food and a place to stay for the night prearranged? What had happened

117

to the love-handled, squeaky clean, overladen and slightly clueless thirty-somethings that had reluctantly joined the GR5 with food for an army? The changes had been so small and incremental that, at the time, I still couldn't quite put my finger on what it was, but setting out that day I felt more at home on the trail than I ever had before. I had grown to be far more certain that we were doing okay, and far less nervous that we were doing it wrong and messing up even by trying to be out here. In less than two weeks we'd gone from simply surviving to happily thriving in the wilderness.

Still, bunk or no bunk and come rain or shine, our bed still lay 7 hours of hiking away, during which we planned to tackle another high-level variant by going over the Mont de la Saxe crest. We only had 14 kilometres to cover, but with a chunky 1597 metres of climbing and a not insignificant 698 metres of descending, it was time to get a move on.

We soon left the gardens of Courmayeur behind and joined a steep but well-made path that zig-zagged upwards through tree lined slopes. Occasional breaks in the trees revealed magnificent views over Courmayeur and the surrounding forested hills and then, as we got even higher, the summit of Mont Blanc itself appeared, dazzling white against the clear sky. We were making excellent time as we went uphill, driven by enthusiasm more than anything else, and somehow completed the 800-metre ascent from Courmayeur to Rifugio Bertone (1989 metres) in less than 2 hours.

Moving so fast, relatively speaking, suddenly gave us a new appreciation of how busy the trail really was, or at least in this section anyway. From the gaggle of camera-toting Hong Kong hikers being led by a French speaking guide to a pair of elderly American gentleman, one of whom had a cigar hanging out of his mouth ("I don't smoke it, I just like the disapproving looks people give me") as he huffed, puffed and sweated upwards, there just seemed to be a lot more people around. This was especially true outside of the refuge where the grassy plateau was practically swamped with visitors. I even had to queue for 15 minutes to refill our bottles at the water point. But then the view was so unbelievably magnificent it was perhaps unsurprising that this plateau was so busy on such a fine day. The entire gigantic, bare rock wall that makes up the south side of the Mont Blanc massif above Courmayeur was on crystal clear display with all of its ridges, spires, crags, peaks, glaciers and snow fields to admire.

It was while we were taking a moment to catch our breath and check our map that a young couple approached us to ask if we'd found the next sign to Rifugio Bonatti yet? Introducing themselves as Alfred and Mary from Texas, they explained excitedly that they too were walking the TMB, an adventure that they (well, Alfred anyway) had wanted to do for ages, and were having a totally awesome time doing it. With beaming smiles, they radiated an infectious, if sweaty, enthusiasm both for the trail and for life in general. In the space of just a five minute chat we discovered that we had much in common, from Alfred sharing my anorak-like interest in hiking gear specifications to Mary and Esther's shared fears about "holding us back". It also turned out that we had been following an almost identical itinerary since Les Houches, including having both just spent the night in exactly the same cheap hotel in Courmayeur, and although we both preferred the idea of using the tent we carried as often as possible we were both booked in for our virgin experience of a refuge at Bonatti that same evening. It was uncanny, as though we had just met our Asian-American alter-egos.

In fact, the only real difference we identified was that we were about to continue uphill onto the Mont de la Saxe high-altitude variant while Alfred and Mary were heading around the 'standard' balcony route instead.

Despite the physical exertion of the next, technically unnecessary, 500 metres of ascent I have to say I was quite giddy with excitement at the prospect. Having already

sampled the view from the grassy plateau at Rifugio
Bertone, with the blue sky showing no real sign of clouding
up and with the guidebook using phrases like "stupendous
panoramic view of the south wall of the Mont Blanc range",
I really couldn't wait to get to the top of this ridge. After 45
minutes of incredibly strenuous, calf-burning hiking it
didn't disappoint.

It's difficult to overstate the near unrivalled
splendour of the view that accompanied us for the next
three hours, which is the total time it took for us to walk
along the length of the ridge once the gradient had eased
from fiendish to friendly. We probably could have done it
in half an hour, but to have done so would have been to race
through one of the highlights of our entire adventure.
Instead we pottered along slowly until we found an ideal
place to prepare lunch, borlotti beans in a self-made tomato
sauce, and then have a post-food doze in the shade of an
avalanche barrier. As we chewed we admired a scene that
encompassed four full days of our TMB experience. Facing
Mont Blanc, to our left was the broad saddle shape of the
Col de la Seigne we had crossed two days previously, while
to our right was the Grand Col Ferret which we planned to
cross tomorrow. In between lay a feast of alpine delicacies
topped with the iconic skyline of the Mont Blanc massif and
underlined with a valley floor carved by glaciers. It was awe
inspiring in the extreme, and was even made that much
more special by the symphony of alpine flora and fauna that
fluttered and whizzed around us.

Reluctantly we began moving again by mid-
afternoon, heading up one final steep slope to reach the Tête
de la Tronche (2584 metres) and from there downhill
towards the Col Sapin (2436 metres). At the Col Sapin we
found ourselves falling into yet another conversation, this
time with an especially fast moving Belgian hiker named
Leo who was trying to complete the entire TMB in just his
5 day vacation. He'd only left the Rifugio Elisabetta (end of
'Day 3' in the guidebook itinerary) that morning and was

aiming to reach the Rifugio Elena (halfway through 'Day 6') before the forecast storms arrived. Initially he had passed us so quickly that we'd barely been able to exchange a breathless "Buongiorno" and, had he not paused to stuff chocolate and bread into his mouth, that would have been the end of our interaction. Still, for the few minutes we managed to keep up with him after leaving the Col Sapin he proved a very interesting companion, telling us about his job at the EU Parliament in Brussels along with various conservation methods in the Alps which he was passionate about. It was a shame we got to spend so little time with him.

It was during our descent from the Col Sapin, as the adrenalin of the Mont de la Saxe crest wore off, that our thighs and feet began to really ache. No matter how beautiful the scenery is, it turns out you can't walk a vertical mile uphill and not pay a price for it eventually. Unfortunately, with the blue skies that we had dozed beneath during the early-afternoon finally starting to give way to foreboding clouds, we knew this was not a time to be hanging about.

Another hour later and we had climbed the short ascent to reach our final col of the day, the Pas Entre Deux-Saints (2524 metres), and began the gradual, winding descent towards Rifugio Bonatti. Although we were very tired by now, as well as concerned about reaching the refuge before the clouds burst, it was difficult not to feel peaceful in the remote setting of this shallow scree-covered valley head. With no other humans in sight and just a handful of scurrying marmots for company, including a heart-stoppingly cute pup, it was another moment to treasure on this wild, high-altitude day.

Rifugio Bonatti came into view just as the rain began, motivating us to make a sore footed dash across the final few hundred metres before practically bursting into shelter and warmth. Formalities followed. We approached the desk, gave our names, confirmed we didn't want a meal, deposited our boots downstairs in the rancid smelling boot room and then followed a friendly hut guardian to our allocated mattresses. It was all new to us, but also so very easy and welcoming. Although there were smaller rooms available in the building, our dortoir was essentially a long wooden hall containing dozens of mattresses, each one pushed up against the next to make two rows along a central aisle. There was also plenty of space in the middle of the hall to put gear, with hooks and drawers etc., and there were various toilet facilities on each level plus warm showers downstairs. It was everything a hiker could need, and more. Perfect in almost every way. There was only one problem. The sudden onset of panic and claustrophobia!

Although a refuge had seemed a great idea from afar while contemplating a night of camping in a thunderstorm, the up-close reality suddenly felt even more frightening than a few lightning bolts. Minutes earlier we had been revelling in the tranquillity and expansiveness of nature, our personal space extending for miles in every direction. It was one of the main reasons we went walking in the first place, to get away from the hustle and bustle. But now there were people and possessions everywhere, conversations flying across the room in countless languages and the background smell of cooking mingled with socks and armpits. We had mentioned to the guardian on the way to our bunks that this was our first ever night in a refuge and he had congratulated us on choosing such a new and spacious one for our first time. "You'll have a much better night here than in many other places" he had said. Somehow, suddenly, it was hard to believe.

I had only slept in a dormitory once before, on a weekend away with my roller hockey team at the age of 16, when I'd literally had to lie awake for 10 hours trying not to soil myself and silently slipping away to the freezing toilet cubicle each time I did. I'd vowed I'd never willingly sleep in one again. Esther, likewise, had also endured some hellish experiences on school and sports trips in dormitories where she'd been teased about the severe eczema all over her face and body, with some children refusing to even be in a room with her. Her eczema had been so severe during childhood that she'd even had to spend 10 weeks living in a hospital ward, alone, when she was just 3 years old. Needless to say, these were experiences we didn't often bring to mind, except now it was all coming back with a vengeance and left us feeling like rabbits trapped in car headlights. The fact we both felt trapped and panicked wasn't a conscious reaction, or anything to do with the refuge and our fellow guests, it was a reflex and something neither of us had expected.

Esther reacted especially strongly and just wanted to get out of there, immediately, before even taking off her pack. We'd spotted several wild campers settling in just a few hundred metres uphill from the refuge and she couldn't see why we weren't outside as well, especially since it was what we would normally do. "What are we doing here? It's already stopped raining. I want to leave" she hissed under her breath. In response, and despite my own anxiety, I tried my best to be the positive and reassuring one, rattling off a whole list of intellectual reasons why we were better off where we were. "It will definitely storm overnight. This break in the rain is only temporary. This will be much, much better. Let's just take a few minutes and settle in". "And it's part of the whole TMB experience" I added uncertainly, having seen such things written on hiking websites in the past.

I wasn't helping though. Esther continued to stand accusingly rigid in front of her mattress, staring angrily at me and repeating her questions. The presence of wild campers nearby was a particularly sore point. We had been under the impression that wild camping was entirely forbidden everywhere in Italy, yet here we were, in Italy, and there were people wild camping within sight of the refuge. "What are we doing here, why are we carrying a tent and expensive hiking gear and not using it?" she continued to ask.

My ill-considered reaction at this point was to get pissed off, the only side-benefit of which was to help me forget my own fears for a moment. It just didn't feel fair. I'd done my best, I'd arranged for us to have a nice warm bed for the night with best intentions, all I'd wanted to do was to keep us safe and warm, and now Esther was in a flap and having a go at me for it. Even after such an inspiring day of hiking, our physical tiredness coupled with our opposite responses to a panic reflex had put us at loggerheads in a flash. We'd gone from singing to swearing in seconds and were now right on the verge of having one of those 'let's not make a scene' arguments, surrounded by people and so hissing and clenching our teeth at each other in place of throwing insults and crockery.

We managed to avoid it though, just about. We agreed to take a few minutes apart to each calm down and then headed off separately to queue for the time-limited, chilly showers (the hot water had run out) with dozens of other stinky hikers. Feeling a little cleaner and more human we then said a brief hello to our bed-mates for the night, a lone Italian man with an impressive beard on my right side and a friendly young Israeli couple on Esther's left. That helped a lot. At least we'd know the names of the people we might accidentally end up spooning with after dark. ("hey Esther, your beard is tickly tonight"…"grazie").

A short while later, after 99% of our fellow guests had assembled downstairs to devour mountains of cheesy stodge in the humid dining room, we headed outside to cook up our lentil pasta in the now intermittent drizzle when who should appear but none other than our speedy Belgian friend Leo carrying his own cooking set. He was looking a little worse for wear. After the rain had set in, he explained, he had decided to cancel his ambition to reach Rifugio Elena. He had then doubled back on himself for several kilometres seeking a more nearby shelter, since he carried no tent, and had somehow, very fortunately, managed to sweet talk his way into a bed at the otherwise full to bursting Bonatti. Apparently they had unfolded an emergency, spring-loaded bunk in the centre of a room of overweight Germans just for him. He was not expecting a quiet night he told us with a sigh, although this wasn't exactly a surprise to him. His experience of refuges amounted to trying to tire himself out so much during the day that he could at least get a little sleep during the noisy, interruption filled hours of darkness. The problem, as he saw it, was that he didn't drink. "Look around you at what everyone is drinking, it's snoring fuel and the culprits are practically comatose by the time the noise begins". As you can imagine, his words did not exactly boost our own optimism.

Over dinner we talked about many things, some light-hearted and some less so and naturally, with Leo working for the EU, Brexit came up. Since we were undertaking our hike just 6 weeks after the UK's vote to leave the European Union, this was not the first time the word 'Brexit' had been mentioned to us. It was the first time, however, that we got to talk about it in any detail and gone beyond hearing a resigned "Aah, Brexit" accompanied by a sad shake of the head. To be honest, I felt pretty sad about it as well. Administratively and bureaucratically I agreed with many others that the EU, just like individual governments, was expensive and inefficient and that significant reform was no doubt needed at many levels. But did the people who voted "Leave" really think that, instead of being part of that reform, the UK would be a significantly better place to live after a costly and divisive referendum, followed by years of finger-pointing negotiations which will probably lead to a similarly inefficient and expensive system but with rules written on paper with a different flag printed at the top? I guess they did, and I really hope they're right.

Far more likely, it seems to me, is that the new system will be almost identical to the old one, with slightly different wording, different colour passports and a handful of headline making differences that people will applaud or complain about to make it seem like real change has happened. The 'Leavers' will say things got better, the 'Remainers' will say things got worse and the reality will be that nothing much changed at all, despite all of the shouting, finger-pointing and eventual hand-shakes that get reported in the media. Or maybe you're reading this post-2019 and I'm completely wrong, in which case, I hope it got better and not worse.

But that's just the administrative side of things and, whichever way you look at it, trying to organise a few hundred million souls is a complicated business. Far more worrying to me at the time was what the 'Leave' result signified about the undercurrent of feeling, and not only in the UK, but across the whole of Europe. I know that many people voted 'Leave' for reasons completely unrelated to immigration, but no-one can deny that nationalism and anti-immigrant rhetoric was rife during the run up to the Brexit vote. Some people were practically frothing at the mouth to pin the blame for everything from large class sizes to NHS waiting times on Jonny Foreigner. "Control the foreigners" they implied "and everything will be better". It may have only been a minority on the ground but the way it was reported made it seem like far more and that is a dangerous thing. Without balanced reporting extreme ideology can start to seem mainstream, people on the fringes of opinion can start to move with the imagined tide and suddenly a minority movement has a frenzied momentum.

For the previous two years we had moved with fluid freedom through countries which, in living memory, had been shooting bullets at each other. Were we really heading back towards that way of thinking? Everyone thinks it's impossible. Some say that even to ask such questions and compare 'Brexit' to fascism, for example, is just woolly-minded, left-wing naivety. "Nobody really wants that so of course it can never happen again" they say. And then one day it does. But if travelling had taught us anything it was that whichever 'bureaucratic necessity' (aka country) the randomness of birth puts someone in, it doesn't change the fact that all people essentially want the same basic things: to be safe, to be happy and to care for their loved ones. The tragic irony is that the people who want to move to a new country and the people that want to keep them out are motivated by exactly the same thing.

Eventually, when the Brexit dust settles, we may end up back in a similar situation financially and administratively, but it might not feel the same and that's what scares me. But if there is a good place to appreciate how similar we all are, and the importance of getting on with each other instead of fighting and becoming possessive about invisible boundaries, then it is on a stormy night in the mountains with people from all over the world hoping for a safe night's sleep, side-by-side. Especially when the alternative is being left outside in the cold.

Speaking of which, just before we turned in ourselves at Rifugio Bonatti, with the sky almost completely dark, a sorry looking young couple arrived looking cold, wet and bedraggled. We watched them hopefully approach the reception desk and then dejectedly turn away, apparently on the point of tears. There really was no more room at the inn. Esther and I shared a look of mutual understanding and compassion, both knowing immediately that we could so easily have been in the same situation. Hiking too late, making no booking for accommodation, at the mercy of the weather....it was precisely our usual approach.

Almost on cue a quiet ripple of thunder zipped across the threatening sky and I felt their pain. All that they could do was head back out into the cold and rain to put up the soggy tent alongside the other wild campers, who had at least pitched up before the rain arrived, while everyone else around them, including us, was heading inside to a warm mattress.

Vital Statistics - Day 13
Start: Courmayeur
End: Rifugio Bonatti
Distance Hiked: 14 kilometres
Hiking Time: 7 hours
Height Gain: 1597 metres
Height Loss: 698 metres

16. Just Hiking In The Rain

Ear plugs and thunderstorms, two basic ingredients that ensure a wonderful night in a mountain refuge dortoir. Snuggling close together as though in a double bed, albeit with strangers bookending the limits of our private space, we had slept very well indeed as a violent storm raged outside. Yes, there had been a fair bit of snoring throughout the night, along with other disturbances, such as when nearby sleepers stumbled away in search of the loos and decided it was a good idea to turn on the lights, but nothing worth complaining about. It had been such a surprisingly restful night that I found myself waking with a greater than usual amount of goodwill towards my fellow man. The dortoir environment, I decided, is a very humbling and levelling experience.

It was during my own nocturnal tottering towards a toilet, navigating by the pale light of a distant stairwell lamp, that this feeling had struck me the most. On either side of my route were sleepers of all nationalities, ages and genders, not to mention the dozens or so more in other parts of the building. There were single men and women, couples, families, groups of friends and all, for the most part, completely unknown to each other. Yet here they were, sleeping just inches apart with all of their gear and valuables available on communal hanging rails, a situation that looks alarmingly vulnerable compared to most of modern society. And yet it works. How wonderful is that! I felt genuinely grateful to have overcome our own personal demons somewhat and experienced it, even if only for one night.

We were some of the last overnight guests to leave the refuge, at around 9 a.m., just as the bedraggled and dejected couple we had witnessed being turned away into the night reappeared. They squelched into the refuge drying room, clothes and gear soaking, lips blue, hands red raw from the cold and looking like they had just endured a horrific time. The rain had sounded hard and violent enough battering the thick and insulated walls of the refuge that I shuddered to think what it would have been like under canvas. We'd had a few bad weather nights ourselves in the Lake District over the years, on one occasion with a blizzard bending the pole of our tent so much that the tent was flattened onto our bodies like a shroud, but last night's storm had sounded worse. Now, rather than being able to wake up and continue their trip, this young couple had been forced indoors seeking respite and I didn't blame them, especially since the weather was still very poor. It's one thing setting out into the rain wearing warm, dry base layers beneath sturdy waterproofs, but it's quite another trying to get going when you're already drenched. The mountains can be dangerous, inhospitable places and these buildings are called 'refuges' for a reason.

We emerged from Rifugio Bonatti into a thick, drizzly mist that ensured practically no visibility of the beautiful peaks we had enjoyed the previous day. Ahead of us lay another 20 kilometres of hiking, including 895 metres of height gain and 1410 metres of height loss, which we expected to take around 6 hours as we passed over the 2537 metres Grand Col Ferret into Switzerland. Our target for the night was a campsite in the village of La Fouly.

The opening 5 kilometres or so involved a relatively level traverse of the southern flank of the Val Ferret which, with infrequent flashes of sun and breaks in the cloud, still yielded up some intermittent views of parts of the Mont Blanc massif. There was even an occasional rainbow to add some colour to the otherwise drab scene, temporarily creating magical little shows of a glacier tongue or rocky outcrop lit up in multicolour. Far less enticing was the darkness that lay ahead of and above us, with an ominous, threatening mass of cloud shrouding the entire head of the Val Ferret. It was clear that we were walking into another storm. After descending a few hundred slippery metres to

130

the valley floor we began climbing on paths that the guidebook described as "an easy walk upvalley to Rifugio Elena", which turned out to be a very inaccurate description in the rain.

The rain was very heavy by the time we started climbing, with strong winds blasting sheets of water into our faces and keeping our gaze fixed firmly onto our feet. Thankfully we were in pretty much full GORE-TEX® rain gear, all except for our hands as we'd only packed lightweight summer gloves which had, by now, taken on the characteristics of a soggy dishcloth. We tried slipping a couple of plastic bags over the gloves to keep off some of the wind and so retain a little feeling in our fingers, but it was a forlorn hope. That ship had sailed.

Due to the sustained rain and the herd of hikers that had left Bonatti before us the paths had all been churned into slippery mush and so the next 2 hours involved us skidding about like new-born giraffes on ice, trying not to faceplant into the inches deep mud. One slow metre at a time we battled uphill, digging in with the tips of our hiking poles to prevent the wind and gravity sending us back down again. On the one hand I found it quite exhilarating, a struggle between my frail body cocooned in a high-tech bin-bag and the unrelenting, unforgiving forces of nature. On the other hand, it was also a bitterly cold, unbelievably slow and exhausting struggle, especially after the first hour when the non-stop heavy rain began to get the upper hand over membrane technology and started seeping into the places where I really didn't want it to go, places which soon grew both shrivelled and soggy.

By the time we reached Rifugio Elena we were hardly able to frame words with our frozen faces, so it was with a groan of mutual agreement that we immediately dived inside hoping to dry off a little and eat our rations in the warm. As you might expect it was already very busy, crammed full of familiar faces from Rifugio Bonatti doing exactly the same thing. With a hundred or so dripping wet hikers occupying a relatively warm room, the result was something akin to a mass sauna. The refuge staff did their best but their valiant battle to mop their sodden floors while also shepherding the stinky hordes away from the restaurant area, where some families were sitting down to pleasant lunches as though the sky wasn't falling down outside, was clearly a lost cause.

We parked ourselves in a couple of spare seats at an already over-occupied table and began tuning in to the buzz around us, hoping to pick up a little weather-related information. Obviously, the storm was the 'hot' topic of conversation. Some people we overhead said it would clear up very soon. Some said it would clear up much later in the day. Others were saying it would not clear up until tomorrow and so were not going to even try the remaining 500 metres of ascent to the Grand Col Ferret. In fact, the only thing that was clear was that nobody really had a clue what was going to happen with the weather. We decided that we might as well continue, but only after a good thaw and rest in the warm. Besides, what else could we really do? A sign pinned to the wall, probably in response to answering the same query hundreds of times already, clearly stated that Rifugio Elena was now fully booked for the night ahead due to the influx of walk-in bookings that morning, and so was Rifugio Bonatti.

Still, we were in no desperate rush to resume our battle with the elements and so ended up passing a good hour or more at Rifugio Elena, eating our lunch and chatting with some of the other hikers we'd sat down next to. It turned out we were in tough company, with two young women who were on leave from the US Air Force and two British lads, one of whom was a serving navy officer and the other who had just left the army. Naturally they were planning to push on into the weather, so of course, for perfectly sensible, chest-puffing, macho reasons, we definitely had to as well.

The rain continued to hammer the ground as we set off but at least the path above the refuge turned out to be rockier, and therefore less slippy, than that below. There was no view to speak of beyond the mist and clouds so it was really just a case of gritting our teeth and putting one foot in front of the other for the foreseeable future. Despite the cold, our GORE-TEX® lined bodies were still sweating hard as we trudged upwards through the mirk, creating a steady stream of humid warmth which I could feel moving over my face as it escaped by my neck and out into the open air. It's at times like these I find myself feeling most alone and vulnerable in the wild, no matter how many people are around. Each person becomes like an earthbound astronaut, encased in a technological, temperate micro-climate which makes the harsh conditions bearable, but which is also isolating. Outside the weather is alive with energy, but within sounds become deadened, sight is narrowed and communication with even nearby partners is hindered.

We crossed over the Grand Col Ferret and entered into Switzerland wrapped in a particularly dense and bitterly cold cloud that reduced visibility to around one metre. I can't say we really marked the moment. We didn't even try to get our camera out from beneath its many layers of waterproof protection. The guidebook spoke of magnificent views reaching back as far as the Col de la Seigne. Personally, I struggled to see Esther a few metres behind me.

As we descended gently into Switzerland the weather began to brighten. We soon left the coldest parts of the cloud behind and started being able to make out a little of our surroundings, green and pleasant grazing land with occasional Alpages and milking stations dotted around. The drizzle had become intermittent and we could even begin to loosen some of our outer protection, letting nature back into our bodies just a little, but enough to feel invigorating after so long resisting the cold and wet.

133

At some point on the two and a half hour descent into La Fouly we were pleased to join company with the two British military hikers, Dave and Dan, who we'd sat with back at Rifugio Elena. It had been almost a week since we'd hiked with anyone else, since crossing the Col de Voza with Rotem before our rest day, but just like last time we found a few new topics of conversation the ideal way to speed up the damp kilometres, especially with such markedly contrasting life paths and experiences.

Esther and I, from the academic path who had chased mortgages and pensions to the point of disenchantment, and Dave and Dan who had enlisted in the forces straight out of school to see the world and push their limits. Not that they could say much about the details of their various deployments, but what was left unsaid probably spoke louder than what was. It was from Dan in particular, who had recently chosen to leave the army, that we got the greatest sense of both pride and pain trying to coexist. Pride at the professionalism of his unit and of the peacekeeping activities he had been involved in, but also pain at the horrors he would never be able to unsee following deployments in Afghanistan and Iraq. He was in no doubt he had made the right choice to leave but he had no idea what would come next for him, hence jumping at the chance to get away and do some hiking with an old school friend on leave. They only had four days to trek from Courmayeur back to Chamonix and, as far as we could tell, were enjoying their evenings drinking and catching up even more than the scenery. It was a window into another world for us and one we were very grateful to have glimpsed.

In what seemed like no time at all, after meandering along wide tracks through the lush landscape, we were entering La Fouly. We easily found the well-signed camping and handed over what seemed like quite a large number of Swiss Francs for the right to pitch our tent in the already busy field. All of the usual amenities were on offer, including a heated common room for tent campers to make use of. Two hours and a couple of very bloated bellies later (we'd gotten a bit overexcited with a kilogram bag of frozen chestnuts we'd found in the village shop) and we found ourselves sitting in the twilight of that common room enjoying a happy 6-way conversation, having been joined first by Dave and Dan and later by Alfred and Mary who had pitched their tent just a short distance from ours.

I've already mentioned how effortlessly we got on with Alfred and Mary and so it continued this evening as well. It was like seeing parts of our own lives reflected right back at us. Alfred, for example, was a high-flying engineering graduate who had been in a well-paid job, but had found himself feeling depressed and convinced there must be more to life than work and money. After lengthy soul-searching he had seized the bull by the horns and had recently resigned, planning to live on his savings for up to a year while he worked out a new direction for himself. Yet, even after just a few weeks, he already felt torn between chasing those intangible 'new directions' and finding another well-paid engineering job. He had an interview lined up when he got home. Mary, in contrast, worked for a multinational company in a job that involved being available 24/7 to coordinate projects involving people on different continents, so video chat meetings in the early hours of the morning were normal for her. It wasn't great, she admitted, but it was safe and thoughts about leaving scared her, although she wanted to support Alfred in his decision as well. It all sounded very familiar to us.

As fascinating as it was for us to hear their stories, they also wanted to know everything about our life on the road in a motorhome for the previous two years. They wanted to know about our motivations for taking off in the first place, the experiences we'd had along the way and the positives and the negatives of life on the road as we saw it. So, we told them, and we tried not to sugar coat it too much either. It's very easy to get blasé when talking about a life of travel and only focus on the dreamy, blissful parts, because that's mostly what people want to hear about.

Just look at the prevalence of the "freedom-at-forty, how you can retire early like we did" blogs on the internet. It's an easy product to sell because it's what people are already semi-conditioned to expect, that the masses have to accept the drudgery of a slow death beaten out to the rhythm of a 9-to-5, while the lucky few break out of the system and live in endless bliss and carefree simplicity. That you need never feel unhappy ever again, all you have to do is "buy our book, follow our investment plan and in 2 years you too will be mortgage free and sipping margaritas in Mauritius. Special offer at $14.95".

Well, as we'd come to learn, the thing about "living your dream" is that after a while the thing that used to be your 'dream' is now your 'life', and it turns out you still have to wash your own pants, wipe your own arse, manage paperwork and deal with the problems that you can't put away in boxes. Yes, "living the dream" meant we had walked away from so much about our 'old lives' that we associated with our previous unhappiness. No more commuting, no more work clothes, no more bureaucratic email ping-pong, no more breakfast meetings (what sadist invented those?), no more annual reviews and action points, no more caring about traffic jams, no more mowing the lawn, no more.....you get the picture. Motorhome living, for us, was thousands of times better than mortgage-and-pension land, and we felt grateful every day that life had worked out the way it had. So far, so good. I have no hesitation in encouraging anyone that gets the chance to have a career break, or "live their dream", to grab the opportunity and go for it without looking back.

Yet there was also another side of the story. When the dust of our rapid getaway had settled and the novelty had worn off to the extent that I could wake up on a Thursday and not immediately think "I would have been in a progress meeting right now, ha ha ha", we noticed that there were still a handful of problems that we hadn't left behind and which still needed dealing with. A significant chunk of our second year in the motorhome, for instance, was overshadowed by some deep-seated relationship troubles that had built up between us. No matter how many pleasant distractions we filled our days with, we were still human and therefore just as prone to pettiness, getting bored and taking things for granted as we'd always been. It may not be what people want to hear, but even "living the dream" we'd still had our bad days, we still felt angry and sad from time to time and we still argued. It may have happened a lot less than before, and we'd at least had the space and time to get to grips with our issues when they arose, but it still happened.

Naturally everyone wants to hear about the mountains and the lakes and the sunsets and all the other good bits, which is great because that's 95 percent of what our life had become. But if "living our dream" had taught us anything it was that real, deep down happiness could only ever come from within, independent of where we are and what we're doing, which is very easy to say but also very easy to forget in the heat of the moment, as we'd find to our cost the very next morning.

Vital Statistics - Day 14
Start: Rifugio Bonatti
End: La Fouly
Distance Hiked: 20 kilometres
Hiking Time: 6 hours
Height Gain: 895 metres
Height Loss: 1410 metres

17. Another New Direction

With our guidebook proclaiming this next short stage to be the easiest of the entire TMB, it was surprising what a trial it turned into. With only 15 kilometres to cover, a paltry 420 metres of ascent and a barely noticeable 565 metres of descent, it would, indeed, be the shortest and least physically demanding of our entire hike so far. Strange then that we had to take a bus to finish it.

Our previous 5 days of hiking, since we'd taken our comfy rest day at Fan-fan's, had been jammed full with challenges and new experiences, not least of which had been meeting and interacting with so many people doing the TMB after hardly speaking to anyone on the GR5. We'd also hiked for another 90 kilometres and climbed the best part of 5 ½ kilometres along the way, sleeping in our tent 3 times, a cheap hotel and then our first experience of a cramped Alpine dortoir. Plus, and perhaps most importantly, apart from our short-lived grumpiness while contemplating spooning with strangers, we'd also stayed pretty 'happy' throughout it all. Sore feet, thunderstorms, sodden clothes, ego bruises, planning balls ups, for the most part it had slid off us like water from a duck's back. Adventure was what we were out here to do and an adventure is certainly what we were having.

Why then did our emotional boiler explode on this, the morning of the easiest day yet? It was almost as though taking away the pressure of another long, tiring day of hiking had allowed our pent-up feelings to burst forth. The only thing it seemed we could agree on was that "this whole fucking thing was a fucking stupid idea and we should have got a fucking motorhome!" Where had this mutual, explosive anger come from? Coming off the back of such a relaxed, sociable and laughter-filled evening made it even more of a shock. As our new friends packed up and left for another day on the TMB, along with most of the other campers, we found ourselves doing our best to avoid each other. At one point we even left the camping in opposite directions which, given that we had no way of contacting each other, made it a minor miracle we found each other again when we calmed down later on.

I've said it before, but I think it bears repeating, hiking with a spouse is very different from going into the wilderness with friends. There's a whole world of shared history and emotional baggage floating about that can turn even the most innocuous and innocent misunderstanding into the spark for a bonfire, even in a soggy field in Switzerland. One minute you can be having a minor disagreement about coloured socks in the laundry and the next minute you can find yourself in the relationship equivalent of a nuclear strike, there's no going back and there are no winners either.

Our initially minor disagreement on this straightforward day of hiking was about which direction we were actually going to go in. Theoretically, today was the day we had planned to 'turn right', leave the TMB and start heading towards Zermatt. Just 10 kilometres or so down the road was the town of Orcieres, the first place we would come to where the TMB and the Chamonix to Zermatt Walkers Haute Route became one and the same, and it was here that we had provisionally planned to make our change of direction, except that now we weren't so sure.

Part of our reluctance to follow through with our 5-day old plan was because, since leaving Fan-fan's, we had spent precisely no time at all investigating the Chamonix to Zermatt route. We hadn't browsed the stages, investigated resupply options, looked up refuges or possible campsites on the map, or done anything else at all in the way of preparation. All we knew was that all of the necessary amenities existed along the route, somewhere. Compared to the almost unthinking ease with which facilities and services cropped up on the TMB, this made actually going through with our change of direction somewhat daunting.

Still, we were tough hikers, weren't we? Surely, we could cope with a little bit of uncertainty about where the shops were. I mean, it wasn't like we'd looked at such things before striding out on the GR5.

Lack of preparation, however, was not the only source of our reluctance to turn right, because the other was my desire to push my limits in another direction. After speaking with Alfred about the remaining TMB stages the previous evening, it hadn't escaped my notice that after the next, easy stage to Champex was a possible variant stage described as the "toughest [crossing] of the whole route", with paths described as "strenuous", a "chaos of boulders" and "a steep slope of grit". Now that sounded like something I didn't want to miss, even though the sound of it made Esther, with her rapidly accumulating fatigue, more than a little nervous.

Now, going to bed thinking that we had agreed a plan, namely to leave the TMB, and then waking up to find that our plan was open for questioning again shouldn't have been such a big deal, especially for us. Our entire adventure so far had been open to modification pretty much from the moment we'd stepped onto a plane at Heathrow airport, so deciding whether to do an extra day on the TMB, or not, before doubling back into Switzerland really shouldn't have been such a big deal.

Unfortunately for us, however, what happened on this particular morning was that our uncertainty about which way we were going in the immediate moment tapped into a much bigger and far-reaching issue. It was such a big issue, in fact, that it was something we wouldn't be able to fully understand until long after this adventure was over, but it was so fundamental to why we got so stressed out that day that I feel it's critical that I mention it here. I think that the simplest way to put it is that this adventure wasn't just a nice walk in the mountains for us, it was also partly our way of justifying our life choices.

Now that sounds very dramatic, but the truth is that ever since Esther and I had walked away from our old lives of career ladders and mortgage payments, there had been a part of us that felt insecure and guilty about having done so. Back 'home' all of our friends continued to work and strive and save and plan for their pensions, and we just didn't. Instead we went walking and cycling and browsing organic supermarkets, simply because we could. We enjoyed ourselves, certainly, but we also still felt a little guilty to be having such a carefree existence, especially when we saw so many problems in the world and all of our peers still seemed so unhappy. Could it be that we were actually now being selfish? Were we wasting our lives? How could it be OK to simply be enjoying ourselves when all of our life conditioning told us that it wasn't. On the contrary, the way we'd always seen it was that life was supposed to be a struggle where, if we tried really hard, we might come out on top with some success to show for it. But if we didn't try hard enough then we'd sink and be lost in mediocre drudgery.

Associating effort and measurable, material achievement with value and self-esteem had been a hard habit to break, much harder than we ever realised at the time of our Alpine adventure. Looking back now, it's clear to see that many of our choices in our motorhome for the first two years of our life on the road were guided by such concerns, and that trying to make sure our "long walk" was suitably challenging was also an example of our insecurity and need to succeed. But we didn't know that's what it was at the time. All we knew was that we felt unprepared to actually leave the TMB but that not following through with our "impressive" hybrid plan also made us feel very, very anxious for some reason. It felt like we were failing.

Before we knew it, we were arguing. We argued about the route for the day and we argued about the route for the rest of the trip. We argued about why we were even hiking and about why we'd even sold our motorhome in the first place. We argued about what we were going to do when we got back from Egypt and had nowhere specific to go and we argued about how much it would probably cost to stay in hotels. Eventually we even argued about the fact we were arguing. In hindsight, of course, none of our apparent 'problems' were really problems at all. It was all in our minds and, because we were anxious for reasons we didn't fully understand, we'd gotten worked up and temporarily forgotten just how lucky we were to have so much freedom in the first place.

Eventually, thankfully, we came back to ourselves and remembered what it was we had told Alfred and Mary only hours earlier, that true happiness can only ever come from within, irrespective of the where and what.

Anyway, amongst all of the hours we spent arguing, reconciling and reviewing what it was we were doing out here in the first place, we also decided to continue on TMB for a while longer and then double back to Switzerland after going over this apparently tough crossing I was so excited about. Partly, I suppose, we went for this option because we had knackered ourselves out, first arguing and then talking, so staying on the TMB for a couple more days was just easier, but it was also because where we headed to next didn't seem to matter so much right now. We'd blown off a lot of steam and knew that, for today at least, there was no such thing as a wrong direction.

All of which, I hope, in a roundabout way, explains why it took us until almost 7 p.m. to complete what the guidebook suggested should have been just 3 hours of gentle downhill hiking to reach the hamlet of Issert. The hiking itself had been pretty enough, plenty of trees and green fields as we plodded down the valley along the river. Less spectacular than the days in France and Italy, but pleasantly lovely nonetheless.

All that remained ahead of us, in order to complete the suggested TMB stage to Champex, was a single, relatively short 400 metre climb. The only one of the entire day. Yet we couldn't face it. It was almost symbolic of our renewed 'enjoy the moment' resolve that we decided to take a bus at this point. So many times in the past, during long hikes, we had "pushed on" to add an extra peak, an extra col or an extra viewpoint to our mental trophy wall, despite it being detrimental to our overall wellbeing.

This time, however, we got on the bus.

Vital Statistics - Day 15
Start: La Fouly
End: Champex
Distance Hiked: 10 kilometres
Hiking Time: 3 hours
Height Gain: 0 metres
Height Loss: 550 metres

18. High Fliers

There are two TMB routes that leave Champex. The standard route, otherwise known as the "bovine" route, is a relatively gentle plod that climbs up and over the Collet Portala (2040 metres). The other way is the high-altitude variant which crosses the 2665 metre Fenêtre d'Arpette and is described as the "toughest" crossing of the entire TMB. Taken together these two options pretty much form a loop, which was perfect for us since it was still very much our intention to get back on our merry way towards Zermatt, via the Walkers Haute Route, just as soon as I'd satisfied myself with a crossing of the Fenêtre. In fact, since the Fenêtre actually forms part of the Haute Route, we could have gone around the bovine route first and then crossed the Fenêtre in the 'correct' Haute Route direction, but the weather dawned so perfectly in Champex that I didn't want to delay a moment longer than necessary.

We were underway by 9 a.m., almost as soon as the sun touched the campsite, and waved farewell to Dave and Dan who were only just emerging from their nests. Alfred and Mary had already set out a good hour or so before us, planning to take the bovine route as part of their TMB, and we'd only just caught them in time to say farewell and good luck, whatever life had in store for them.

Initially the trail out of Champex wasn't too challenging, just beautiful. It was already hot, surrounded by spruce and fir trees, so we were very grateful for the refreshingly cool breeze coming off the fast-flowing water which sluiced through irrigation channels carved alongside the trail. After only about three quarters of an hour among the trees we emerged into a clearing by the refuge Relais d'Arpette. Looking ahead, beyond a long meadow hemmed in on both sides by more trees, was the impressive sight of the lofty Dents du Midi set against the bright blue morning sky. It was an idyllic mountain outlook, with the green bowl of the valley framing the distant grey peaks.

We were about halfway along the meadow when we suddenly became aware of a loud crashing sound coming from the tall, bamboo-like grass on our left. Our reflex response was to freeze. "Is it a wild boar?" we whispered. "Do they even have those here?" We were entirely alone at this point, having seen no other hikers since setting off, and the crashing was getting louder and louder as though it was coming directly for us. Soon enough we could see the tops of the long grass thrashing around as though being trampled by something big and heavy, slow moving but still coming straight for us. "Maybe we should make some noise" I suggested, "to scare it off before it gets to us". "Ok" Esther agreed. So we started jumping up and down, making a racket with our sticks on the floor and "Ooo Ooo" noises at the top of our voice, like two oversized howler monkeys. The creature didn't stop though, if anything it moved faster, and then it did something even more surprising because it said "Erm, hello" in a voice that sounded just like Alfred's.

Sure enough, after only a few more seconds of thrashing, our friends emerged, sweating and flustered, from the jungle of grass. Apparently, they'd had a last-minute change of heart and had decided to try going over the Fenêtre d'Arpette after all, but had then lost their way after being flummoxed by an electric fence strung out across the trail, the same one which we'd passed through a short while beforehand.

I'd never really considered it before, but while we had grown used to passing through gates and over stiles in the UK, as well as elsewhere in the Alps, as polite and respectful Americans in Europe for the first time, Alfred and Mary had been highly unsure what to do. Their guidebook told them to go forward but the fence implied that the field ahead was private property......so instead they had spent the last hour scrambling through dense trees and long grass more akin to the Bolivian jungle than the TMB. Needless to say, they looked a little worse for wear.

It was a happy reunion, the first chance we'd had to actually walk with Alfred and Mary. Pretty soon though the path began to kick sharply upwards and Alfred and I, maintaining a surprisingly brisk pace, unnecessarily forged quite a long way ahead. We reunited half an hour later, where Mary said she felt like taking a short break. Whether that was a tactful way of saying "stop racing you macho morons", I didn't ask, but we all wished each other well and looked forward to getting together again at the top or, failing that, the camping at the end of the day.

Up, up and up we went, entering into a deep groove in the landscape created by the valley wall on our right and a huge glacial moraine on our left. Up ahead we could see that the valley forked, with this moraine emerging from the meeting point of the two arms, and could just about imagine two enormous glaciers coming together over the millennia to leave this giant heap of rubble hidden beneath them. We were moving surprisingly fast, spurred on by the sunshine and adrenalin of the moment, and were soon looking down on a far distant Alfred and Mary still enjoying their break.

Leaving the treeline below, we entered into boulder fields and scree slopes as the trail skirted beneath the Dents du Midi and then followed the right-hand fork of the valley. Increasingly the path became rockier and wilder until, by the time we reached the foot of the final, especially steep part of the ascent, we were unsure if there was even an actual 'path'. Every now and then we caught sight of a red and white mark spray-painted onto a rock, but it was difficult to string enough sightings together to follow a particular route. Instead we simply negotiated ourselves over, around and sometimes even under the overhanging portions of giant boulders in what seemed to be the right general direction. Up above we could now see a few other hikers doing the same thing, but everyone seemed to be taking their own unique route. It was a case of every hiker

146

doing their best to stay safe and ascend in whatever footsteps they saw fit. This was real, wild hiking and it was exhilarating.

Finally, we arrived. It had been a gruelling three hour ascent beneath an increasingly hot sun, but it definitely was, as the guidebook said, "a highlight of the route in every sense". Looking ahead and down we were confronted with the deep and green Vallée du Trient running into the far distance, with countless other snow-capped peaks making up the northern skyline. To our left, the sweeping Trient glacier looked enormous and brilliant blue in the midday sun, emerging from a bright white snow field before extending its now sadly shortened tongue down into the valley which it had helped to carve. Looking back, the route we had just climbed provided an entirely different scene, with the scree coated Val d'Arpette pointing towards the snowy Combin massif in the east.

Physically this had definitely been the hardest ascent so far, but with cloudless blue skies and barely any breeze we felt so grateful to have chosen this route. The Fenêtre d'Arpette itself was an incredibly narrow col made up of just a couple of steep, muddy banks and lots of large boulders. Given the time of day, and the monumental views, we decided we'd join the couple of dozen other hikers that were already lounging around the top and began to seek our own lunchtime perch, but it proved somewhat tricky finding a patch of ground that was sufficiently flat that we could put our bags down without them starting the descent without us. In the end we had to tie them to our feet.

We lingered for the best part of an hour and a half in the hot sun at the Fenêtre d'Arpette. Partly it was such a beautiful place that we just didn't want to leave, but we also wanted to wait for our friends to arrive so that we could enjoy this incredible place together. Yet they just didn't appear. Eventually we decided it was time for us to get going, hoping our friends would arrive soon for their own sake as we had grown more than a little concerned that

147

something had happened to them. Looking as far as we could back into the Val d'Arpette we couldn't make out any moving shapes that looked like Alfred and Mary at all. "They left the camping 5 hours ago now. They should be here really. Maybe they turned back?" we guessed.

The way downhill was less technically difficult than the way up had been, but in the roasting afternoon sun the effort required felt double. Fortunately, we had the Glacier du Trient, or what was left of it, for company the whole way down. Over the next two hours we went from being up close with ice and boulders while looking down on a distant valley floor, to sitting among wild flowers and looking up at a tiny smudge of blue-grey ice that we knew to be the Trient glacier. It was beautiful. Even the extensive, smoothed rock surfaces that acted as a reminder of the now vanished portions of glacier had their own special artistry although, as always, they did make us feel saddened at the thought that one day, probably within our own lifetimes, all of the ice would be gone.

Our overnight destination, a field outside of a gite d'etape which allowed camping in the village of La Peuty, was another 45 minutes down the valley. For the princely sum of 2 CHF each (about £1.50), plus an extra 2 CHF so that we could use the toilets and warm showers beneath the nearby gite, we had everything we could wish for, or mostly anyway. The field was busy, but not overly so, and our front door opened onto the now distant sight of the Glacier du Trient. We even had a picnic bench to prepare and eat our dinner on.

The air cooled fast once the sun dipped behind the mountains and we found ourselves sat in the shade, cooking our buckwheat noodles and gazing up at the still sun-soaked glacier. It was hard to believe just how fast we had gone up and over the col, and it hardly seemed real that just a few hours earlier we had been right up there among the mountain tops.

148

As evening wore on we found ourselves chatting to other nearby campers as they arrived, all of whom were also nearing the end of their TMB experiences. One Bulgarian couple, Lazlo and Dorka, upon hearing about my medical reasons for why we'd started travelling, shared that they had a young daughter with an almost identical bowel condition to me and said that they felt encouraged to see me living such a full and active life. They worried about her future and how much she would be able to do as she got older. It was another reminder of how similar we all are underneath, just wanting the best for our loved ones regardless of where we all come from. Maybe that was the real beauty of hiking and exposing ourselves to our own vulnerability by going into the wild. It can remind us that, compared to the forces of nature, we are all equally powerless, no matter how much influence we think we have within our fleeting human creations.

And, speaking of vulnerability, exactly where were Alfred and Mary? It had been almost ten hours now since we'd left them taking a break on a rock on the other side of the col. Now, with headtorches being lit and tents starting to get zipped up for the chilly night ahead, we were seriously starting to regret not exchanging phone numbers earlier in the day. They'd been on the go for almost twelve hours by now and we were even wondering at which point we might consider phoning mountain rescue. "Surely, we can't do that. It was a busy enough path, wasn't it? I mean, if something had happened, they'd have been seen and gotten help already, wouldn't they?"

And then, out of the twilight, we saw the shape of two figures moving quickly towards the field. "Could it be?", "I think it is", "It's them" we shouted as Alfred held his arms aloft in triumph. They had arrived, 11 ¾ hours after they had left Champex. We clapped and cheered as they got closer, as did several other nearby groups who joined in simply for the fun of it, and then we sat down

149

together to relive some of the splendour of the day in the dying light of the evening.

Vital Statistics - Day 16
Start: Champex
End: La Peuty
Distance Hiked: 14 kilometres
Hiking Time: 6 ½ hours
Height Gain: 1199 metres
Height Loss: 1139 metres

19. Dash For The Line

Morning dawned to the sound of cockerels crowing and hiking poles ticking along the nearby road. With the sun only just beginning to poke out above the high ridges around us it was still bitterly cold in the valley bottom, yet by the time we opened our tent flap we were almost entirely alone. The only people not yet awake, it seemed, were Alfred and Mary, their still silent tent suggesting they needed a lie in of their own.

Mopping up puddles of condensation as best we could, we rolled away our sodden tent and prepared to leave. Breakfast, such as it was, was a brief and unsatisfying affair involving just a few hundred grams of oats and some lukewarm water. We were now out of both food and fuel. We knew that there was a store of some kind in La Peuty, but it didn't open for another two hours which felt like far too long to wait. France, and the remainder of the TMB, was calling.

Abandoning our plan to loop back to Champex via the "bovine" route wasn't something we had especially discussed. If Zermatt was our ultimate destination then that was still the only direction that made sense, but for some reason we just sort of woke up and knew that we were going to follow the TMB for at least one more day. We knew it was the 'wrong' direction as far as Zermatt was concerned, but still we just shouldered our packs and headed in the same direction as the crowds. This time we didn't have to discuss it.

Just before leaving the campsite we did get a chance to say (another) final farewell to Alfred and Mary, who appeared out of their tent only moments before we began to march. Now this was an emotional moment. It may have only been five days since we'd first encountered each other in the hot sun above Courmayeur, but with so much in common and now a raft of shared experiences, we had

151

grown very close in a very short time. It was the only genuinely difficult goodbye of our entire adventure.

Our final border crossing of the TMB, from Switzerland back into France, would involve a 900 metre climb to the Col de Balme. The path out of La Peuty was initially steep, zig-zagging uphill through a forest, and for no good reason we found ourselves power walking, taking long strides and driving our hiking poles into the ground like cross country skiers. Despite being some of the last to leave the camping at the pace we were going we were soon passing other groups of hikers like we were trapped on an out of control Stairmaster. It was exciting, and entirely pointless, but who cared. We were awake, alive and racing through the Alps. We didn't even really know where we were going since our 'plan' had been to go in an entirely different direction, but in the moment what more did we need? We were moving for the sheer joy of it.

Many of the faces we nodded and smiled at as they flashed past were the same familiar faces we had been nodding and smiling at for much of the past week. There was the Israeli couple we had practically slept with back at Rifugio Bonatti for instance, and then, a short while later, the two American gentleman we had first spoken to climbing out of Courmayeur and who flagged us down for another chat as we drew level with them.

John and Michael were their names and we learned that they had wanted to experience the TMB for years, but just hadn't had the time before their retirement. Now, with just a couple more days remaining until the finish, they were raving about how wonderful everything had been for them so far. The food, the people, the scenery. It had all surpassed their expectations and yet, looking back, they had to admit that one of the most powerful experiences had come when they least expected it.

As Americans, still living in the apparently perpetual shadow of 9-11, they couldn't pretend that there wasn't an undertone of suspicion "back home" regarding Muslims and people from the Middle East in general. It wasn't racism per se they felt, but they were aware of a definite uneasy vibe in the circles they moved in. And then, a few days earlier, while the rain had been lashing down hard over the Grand Col Ferret, they had decided to avoid the rain and travel instead in the support van which their tour organiser used to move their luggage to their next overnight destination. What they didn't know, since they'd always started hiking before their bags were collected on previous days, was that the driver who moved the luggage just so happened to be from the Middle East. Spending a couple of hours side by side with someone who they might otherwise have avoided, just in case, had apparently "opened [their] eyes". It turned out they had a lot in common, particularly a love of nature and a focus on family. Reminders like this, that everyone is motivated by the same things underneath our superficial differences, just seemed to be cropping up everywhere.

The final approach to the Col de Balme was over much more open hillside and we found ourselves baking in the now hot sun. Stepping out of Switzerland and back into France at 2191 metres, we were presented with a stupendous view along the Chamonix valley. Unlike any other perspective we'd enjoyed so far, this was the best angle yet for appreciating the elongated ridge shape of the complete massif, with countless peaks and troughs visible against the clear blue sky. Before the TMB I had always pictured Mont Blanc as a 'peak' but in reality it is only one summit at the end of an enormous strip of undulating mountainside, albeit the highest of the crowd.

We soon left the col and descended the grassy hillside for a couple of hundred metres to reach another broad plateau, and then up again to cross the Aiguillettes des Posettes ridge at 2201 metres. As we walked the view to our left of the looming Mont Blanc massif changed ever so gradually, with different crevasses and glaciers slipping in and out of sight. All that stood between us and one of

Europe's most iconic panoramas was several miles of clear Alpine air filling a deep green valley. It was amazing.

After leaving the sharp ridge a steep and winding descent followed, with just a few straggly trees available to offer shade from the now punishing sun. With gravity on our side we continued to maintain the fast pace we'd been setting since leaving camp, arriving into the hamlet of Tré-le-Champ practically at jogging pace. It was only just past midday and somehow we had just completed what was supposed to be 5 hours of hiking in just 3 hours, and it hadn't felt like a strain at all. Suck on that Paddy!

We were getting a little peckish though and, since we soon discovered that there was no 'food' available, other than soft drinks, chocolate and ice cream at the Auberge in Tré-le-Champ, we suddenly found ourselves in a bit of a quandary. It was now early afternoon and, technically, adding up the remaining portions of TMB standing between us and the Col du Brévent we were only 6 hours away from completing the entire Tour de Mont Blanc. At the rate we'd been moving we could probably do that before dark. It was a tempting proposition, not because we were in a particular rush or even that bothered about completing it at all, but simply because it was a challenge and we were currently unsure what else we were doing. On the other hand, we also had no food or fuel left and, even if we did make it to the Col du Brévent before dark, we'd still be close to 2500 metres and need to find somewhere safe to camp. We knew it didn't add up.

Resolving to resupply with food and fuel as soon as we could and then reassess, we temporarily left the TMB and resumed our rapid downhill marching, following the river to reach the busy town of Argentière. We knew, with cast iron certainty, that there would definitely be a supermarket here. What we hadn't counted on, however, was that it would be closed for lunch when we arrived.

It was after 4 p.m. by the time we had caught a bus back up to the TMB trail at the Col des Montets, a little above the hamlet of Tré-le-Champ. We could have walked back from Argentière, but carrying an enormous honeydew melon, several cucumbers, some cooked beetroot and a lentil based ready meal, our heart just wasn't in it. Whatever had been driving us to move so quickly all morning had ebbed away during the time we'd spent lounging around in Argentière waiting for the shop to re-open. We were feeling more than a little drowsy as we sat down to enjoy our first real meal of the day. By now we were so hungry that, once again, we went a little overboard. By the time we felt able to stand up without belching it was half past five and our shadows were already getting noticeably longer.

Our chosen destination from the Col des Montets was the high-altitude Refuge Lac Blanc at 2351 metres, a further 1000 metres of climbing above our heads and another variant from the standard TMB route. Our motivation for going up there was simply that it was described as having "one of the finest of all alpine views that can be enjoyed", with a picture included in the guidebook to suggest this was not an exaggeration. Also, rather than taking the most direct route to the refuge by following the standard TMB at least two thirds of the way before deviating higher, we had decided to take a different variant the entire way. Our chosen route wasn't supposed to take very much longer timewise but did require a much steeper initial ascent followed by a long and undulating traverse along the "Grand Balcon Sud", a route famed for offering a perfect and high-altitude vantage point from which to appreciate the peaks and glaciers of the northern face of the Mont Blanc massif. With a perfect evening developing in the sky above our heads, if all went according to plan then the next few hours of our adventure promised to be some of the most picturesque of all.

The opening section of the climb was indeed very demanding, with short, dusty zig-zags criss-crossing the hillside. Unfortunately for us the zip and zing had definitely vanished from our legs, turning what may have been a light-hearted skip uphill earlier in the day into a slightly belligerent, foot-scuffing trudge. Not that there weren't abundant rewards on offer for our efforts. Being up on the Grand Balcon Sud late enough in the day to have it almost to ourselves was a far more magical experience than we could have ever imagined, with one iconic view of Mont Blanc and its neighbours after another. We also found ourselves, on several occasions, surrounded by large family groups of ibex, evidently quite used to the sight of human snails plodding through their back garden and so unafraid of our relative closeness. Our cuteness meter almost burst when we came across an adult pair protecting a nursery group of five young, each lounging nonchalantly on a rock to soak up the final rays of the day. It felt like we had hiked into a lost world, a private and visually stunning realm that belonged, for a short while at least, only to us.

By the time we started to negotiate the undulating traverse portion of the route we were moving incredibly slowly. Partly this was because we were knackered, but also partly because we just kept stopping to take photos. We knew we needed to move faster, with the sky already developing a pinkish hue, but the scenery just kept begging to be appreciated.

By the time we reached Lac Chéserys at 2200 metres it was almost 9 p.m. and we knew that we didn't have the time, or energy, remaining to complete the final 150 metres of ascent to Refuge Lac Blanc. Instead we immediately found a spot just large and flat enough to park our tent and knackered bodies for the night. Even though we could race through the necessary tasks on autopilot by now, our respective jobs perfectly choreographed as we unfolded, inflated and pegged-out in sync with each other, it still took almost all of our remaining energy to get the job done. Finally, with stars starting to appear in the sky, we settled down to a final, simple meal of the day. The day had started with and would also end with porridge.

More importantly, however, we were alone. I'm not saying that the previous four nights since arriving at Rifugio Bonatti hadn't been charming, chatting and laughing with others, but being back in the hills and entirely on our own again just felt right. Probably more so precisely because we'd been with others. In fact, come to think of it, we hadn't had a pitch like this since we'd crossed the Col d'Anterne on our sixth day. It had been busy campsites, refuges and rooms ever since.

Now, with just the damp grass, lapping waters of the lake and the starry silhouette of Mont Blanc for company, it felt like we'd come home.

Vital Statistics - Day 17
Start: La Peuty
End: Lac Chéserys
Distance Hiked: 17 kilometres
Hiking Time: 7 ½ hours
Height Gain: 1800 metres
Height Loss: 1000 metres

20. Checking Out, Checking In

The story of the night was that we slept in a cloud and awoke to the sound of hard rain rapping on our tent. Just before bed I'd ventured out onto some exposed hillside to perform my first nocturnal outdoors enema in a while and had been startled by some voyeuristic Ibex. Fortunately, they seemed happy just to watch. And then the rain had arrived and maintained a steady, persistent drumming all night long.

It was just after 7 a.m. when we ventured outside to discover a much finer view than we had could ever have hoped for, with much of the Mont Blanc massif still visible through the drizzly rain. Gone, however, were the white snowy peaks and the blue glacial ice falls, framed by green trees and beige, sun-baked grass. Instead the tops of the peaks were hidden and the snow and ice that could be seen had turned countless shades of grey.

Given the weather, we immediately abandoned our pre-sleep plan to tackle the additional 150 metres of ascent to Lac Blanc in order to enjoy "one of the finest of all Alpine views" for ourselves. Getting off the mountainside before the really heavy rain returned seemed a much more sensible plan of attack, or should that say graceful retreat?

It took us only an hour of soggy striding to reach the Refuge la Flégère at 1875 metres altitude. By now the rain was stopping and starting in heavy bursts, and the looming clouds seemed to be sagging even lower in the sky. Officially, from this refuge, we still had another 2 ½ hours of hiking with 300 metres of uphill before we would formally 'complete' our personal version of the TMB at the Col du Brévent, but all we could see of the trail ahead of us was mist and cloud. We still talked about doing it though, now that we were so close and all. Probably, if we'd actually started our walk at Les Houches like most people tackling the TMB seemed to, then we would have continued

158

on and done the final 6 ½ hour stage just to say that we did it, rain or no rain. The problem was, we already knew what it was like at the top of Le Brévent in good weather.

In the end we just couldn't summon up the enthusiasm to walk inside of a cloud for the sake of it and we decided to call it a day. Two hours of downhill hiking later and we found ourselves leaving the muddy trail behind and stepping back into the realm of concrete civilisation, reaching the outskirts of the bustling town of Chamonix. In terms of culture shock, the transition from waking in idyllic solitude on the shores of Lac Chéserys, to queueing in the thronging Chamonix tourist office during an August lunchtime was pretty challenging. It was the smell I noticed first. Not the smell of other people, I'm not that much of a hypocrite, but the smell of traffic. It really stuck in the back of my throat. After more than 2 ½ weeks, with just a few small towns and villages to break up the natural environment, this was a very different prospect. Even Courmayeur hadn't come close. Not that there weren't some benefits, like heating and cushioned seats, for example, but I wasn't sure they were a price worth paying for allowing my personal space to be so rudely violated.

Damp, smelly and muddy, we piled our bags on a bench and tried to keep our elbows by our sides so as not to make anybody flinch. Not that we needed to worry too much. Although it was true that most of the queuing tourists looked to be quite well-heeled sightseers, we weren't the only unshaven, sunburnt and slightly whiffy hikers cluttering up the place and, like us, most of them looked a little lost. Not lost in the sense of not knowing where they were, but lost in the sense of "what do we do now that we've finished?" Personally, I was aware of a strong sense of both relief and disappointment that our TMB was now over, the love-child of which was a mild sense of anxiety.

Eventually the queuing was over and, armed with a list of hotels where we might find a not unnecessarily expensive room for the night, we headed out into town to make some calls. In the end the hotel we chose, the 3-star Hotel du Bois in Les Houches, was neither the cheapest or most convenient, but it was the hotel that had allowed me to use their toilet during our first visit to Les Houches 11 days earlier. I'd walked in, flustered and rushed, and they'd kindly shown me the way to their foyer bathroom and then put up a sign to redirect other guests elsewhere while I used it. Handing our 70 euros over to them, instead of another random hotel, just felt like a good way of saying thank you. Plus, with the free bus service which runs along the Chamonix Valley available to anyone staying in the area, we knew we could reach it easily.

We didn't hop straight on the bus though. Although we still anticipated another 8 or 9 days of hiking through the Alps towards Zermatt, some form of celebration to mark our 'completion' of the TMB seemed to be in order, and we weren't the only ones. No sooner had we toasted our fine and smelly selves with a small bottle of kombucha from an organic épicerie, when we spotted John and Michael, the American gentleman, doing exactly the same with a glass of beer just down the street. We wished them congratulations and good luck for their future adventures. Then, wandering along to catch a bus, we literally collided with Laszlo and Dorka enjoying their own final day in the area. Our short time wandering along the busy streets of Chamonix was beginning to feel a little like a farewell party, I just wasn't sure what it was we were saying farewell to. We hadn't finished yet.

By mid-afternoon we were showered and were inspecting our trail battered bodies in our comfortable hotel room. Rashes, insect bites, bruises, blisters, peeling skin.....we didn't think we'd come off too badly. Certainly nothing that a hearty organic salad and fermented food feast from Les Houches' organic supermarket, 200 metres down the road, couldn't put right, followed by a bloated float about in the pool and a sauna for good measure. Sitting together in the heat, romantically sloughing off handfuls of flaking skin from our backs, bellies and thighs, it was a moment to treasure, in a good way.

We were so excited (and not just by the quantity of skin we'd gotten rid of) that we quickly decided to stay at the Hotel du Bois for 2 nights instead of just 1. Not only did it make the room slightly cheaper per night, but the prospect of just not having to relocate the next morning was enticing. It had already been 8 days since our only other rest day so far, at Fan-fan's, and now seemed like the perfect time to have another. A rest was surely what we needed to re-energise before tackling the Haute Route into Switzerland.

Vital Statistics - Day 18
Start: Lac Chéserys
End: Chamonix / Les Houches
Distance Hiked: 5 kilometres
Hiking Time: 2 ½ hours
Height Gain: 0 metres
Height Loss: 1200 metres

21. They Think It's All Over, It Is Nearly

Eating, sitting and lying down filled the bulk of our second rest day, along with a few other necessary jobs like washing our clothes and swimming in the pool, just because we could. We also revisited our route planning. Ever since we'd decided to leave the GR5 at the Col de la Croix du Bonhomme, it had been our ultimate intention to pick up Chamonix to Zermatt Walkers Haute Route. Yet several times now, when we'd had the chance to do so, we had turned away. First we'd caught a bus to the camping at Champex, when the more direct option in terms of the route to Zermatt would have involved getting off the bus elsewhere. Then we'd crossed the Fenêtre d'Arpette, promising ourselves that we'd loop back around towards Zermatt the very next day. And then we'd crossed the Col de Balme and returned to France. Quite why we had done this we still weren't sure, but now that we had run out of TMB it was time to get our heads out of the sand. What exactly were we going to do with our remaining ten days in the Alps?

Our initial assumption was that we would, somehow or other, get back on terms with the Walkers Haute Route and still get as close to Zermatt as we possibly could. The complete Walkers Haute Route is a 187-kilometre undertaking that can be completed in roughly 12 – 14 days, at a good pace, so it was definitely still a possibility for us. We only had ten days left until our flight left Geneva, but we had already completed (pretty much) the first 2 days of the route in reverse. Provided we could get back to Champex, we could probably still do much of the route as it was laid out in the associated guidebook.

We set about bashing out the detailed logistics using another of Kev Reynolds' masterpieces, also published by Cicerone guides. Was there a bus, or buses, we could take back into Switzerland? How long would our hiking stages be? Would we try and stay in refuges or would we try and wild camp? And, if we were going to camp, where would we do it since it is officially discouraged in Switzerland? How often would we be able to buy food and so how much would we need to carry? There was a lot to think about. These were issues we hadn't even attended to before embarking on the GR5, so at least our experience so far had us asking the right questions.

We'd been really quite fortunate on the GR5 that we had set off naively and somehow gotten away with it so well. What we'd needed had just seemed to appear, almost magically at just the right times, and this had been supported with a few important changes in our own outlook so that we hadn't been too bloody minded to ask for help or change our plans when necessary. Then, on the TMB, since it is pretty much the most popular walking route on the planet, we really hadn't had to worry about very much at all. We'd overdone it a couple of times, but the TMB was so well serviced by amenities it hadn't seemed to matter. In contrast, the Walkers Haute Route that we were about to attempt still seemed a far more remote and daunting option.

Some of the stages suggested in the guidebook were shorter than many of our days so far, but others were more strenuous and the terrain sounded far more wild, staying at very high altitude for long periods and even with the possibility of some ice crossings. Esther was already getting concerned about her current level of fatigue being more than just tiredness and was mindful that she might be on the verge of another ME relapse. For myself, although I'd just about managed it so far, I really wasn't madly keen on the prospect of another ten days of outdoor enemas. Yet, despite all of that, it was still the most enticing prospect we could come up with, and we really did want to go back to Switzerland. Even if we were willing to accept we'd overdone it somewhat, tiredness and nerves, to us, still didn't seem like good enough reasons to go back on a plan. We'd come out here to do a month of hiking, and a month of hiking was what we were going to do. What else was there?

After taking a good long while to digest the stages and plan out an itinerary that we thought would suit our needs, we just about managed to calm our reservations.

Eventually, as bedtime approached, we had somehow managed to psych ourselves up to leave creature comforts behind yet again, ready for one more push which would take us out into the wildest section of our adventure so far.

And then, just when we thought we knew what lay ahead, we got an email that had the potential to change everything.

Vital Statistics - Day 19
Start: Les Houches
End: Les Houches
Distance Hiked: 0 kilometres
Hiking Time: 0 hours
Height Gain: 0 metres
Height Loss: 0 metres

22. A Farewell Salute to the Wild

As had been our habit for much of the adventure, having gone to bed with a decision to make that could drastically change our entire plan, we woke up and decided to put off thinking about it for as long as possible. Instead we decided to take as much advantage as we could of our hotel by heading back to the pool, sauna and steam room for most of the morning, eventually checking out a little while after the official eviction hour. Only then did we set up camp in a quiet corner of the hotel bar and settle down to make our big decision.

This was our conundrum. The previous evening we had been mentally preparing ourselves for the Walkers Haute Route, an option which would have meant at least another 8 days of thru-hiking through the beautiful Swiss wilderness, before hopping onto buses and trains in order to get back to Geneva in time for our flight. It would mean heavier packs than before, due to the sparsity of shops, and probably also a lot more wild camping, since we had made no reservations and other than mountain refuges, accommodation options were few and far between. It would be beautiful, certainly, but after almost three weeks of trail life we had to admit we were more than a little fatigued. Well, strictly speaking we didn't have to admit it because we didn't like to admit such things, but it was still a fact that we were tired. Whether we would have been quite so tired if we'd approached our hike so far a little more sensibly was debatable, but dealing in 'ifs-and-buts' wasn't going to help much, was it?

Alternatively, we could go and spend the week before our flight living in a luxury apartment in one of our favourite places on earth. Now that was an option we hadn't seen coming at all.

We'd first met Shirley and Robin two years earlier, during our very first visit to the beautiful Val d'Anniviers in

Switzerland. It had been a chance meeting, on a hike incidentally, and at first we'd only talked for perhaps ten minutes while standing by a mountain stream in the quiet of the morning sunshine. We'd said farewell and gone our separate ways, but just a short while later the heavens opened and we found ourselves dashing back to the nearest cable car station and riding a plastic bubble back to warmth and dryness together. Then they'd invited us back to their apartment for tea and biscuits.

Ever since that first meeting we'd stayed in touch. They were such kind, goodhearted people who told us about many of their own favourite walks and sights in the Val d'Anniviers, a place we would go on to fall head over heels in love with ourselves. Of all the many mountain locations we had visited during our first year on the road, Val d'Anniviers was the only one we had gone back to more than once. It was everything we had ever dreamed of finding. Quiet, remote, beautiful, covered in hiking trails, green in summer and golden in autumn. Frankly, had it not been for the winter cold setting in, we may never have left at all. Oh, and it also happens to lie directly on the Chamonix to Zermatt Walkers Haute Route.

Having committed to setting out on the Haute Route the next morning, just before bed we had decided to email Robin and Shirley to let them know we'd be passing through their area in a week or so and would love to say hello, if they were at home. They'd replied quickly, as they always did, to say that sadly they were currently in the UK so couldn't meet up. However, they did offer, very generously and unexpectedly, to rent us their apartment for a week if we wanted it, even sending us a link to tantalise and remind us what is was like (http://www.grimentzswitzerland.co.uk). This was the Option B that had suddenly been placed on the table just before we went to bed. What were we going to do?

Intellectually the sensible option was to take the apartment, we knew that almost immediately. It was such a great offer and we really were getting very tired. Getting to stay in an apartment and take shorter, easier day hikes over the hills of the magnificent Val d'Anniviers seemed like a wonderful way to still get out on the hills, but without continuing to break our bodies more than necessary. Also, in just over a week and half we'd be getting on a plane to what we both hoped would be another fantastic adventure, an all-inclusive trip to Egypt in five-star luxury. We'd never done anything like it before. Did we really want to arrive in Cairo feeling sleep deprived, physically exhausted and still smelly from the trail, when we could arrive refreshed and clean?

Yet letting go of our Haute Route plan was so very hard. Walking away, right at the moment that we were poised to re-join the trail meant, essentially, admitting that we were choosing comfort over adventure. It wasn't that we 'couldn't' do it, but that we just didn't want to as much as we wanted to relax. We still loved the mountains and the great outdoors, but over the course of the previous 2 ½ weeks a new concept had also started to creep into our awareness, the idea that we didn't actually want to live out of rucksacks indefinitely. Probably a good term for what we were feeling was "travel method fatigue". During our very first year of motorhome travel it had taken us 10 months of living in a big, rolling tupperware before we'd admitted we were starting to crave a little more space. As a result, we had ended up renting what was essentially a 2-bedroom shed on a Spanish campsite for 2 months, complete with our own shower cubicle and ceramic toilet. It had re-energised us and, by the time we had moved back into our motorhome, we were raring to go again. What we were feeling out here in the Alps was a similar craving for a change, except this time it had come on alarmingly swiftly. As much as my tough guy ego might have anticipated, or even wanted, to be able to live in the wild indefinitely, my comfort-seeking instincts were in rebellion.

It was a long and winding discussion, tucked away in the corner of the bar of the Hotel du Bois, but as much as our egos resisted I think that they knew the writing had been on the wall for our hike ever since Shirley and Robin's unexpected offer arrived in our inbox. All they really needed was to feel heard, so that when we did make the decision to accept their kind offer it wasn't as though they had given in too easily. Or perhaps that's just what our egos needed to tell themselves. Either way, by the time we left the Hotel du Bois it was no longer the Walkers Haute Route that we were heading for, it was a comfortable apartment the Val d'Anniviers.

It was now Thursday afternoon and the stay that had been offered in the Val d'Anniviers would run from Saturday to Saturday. That meant we still had 2 nights left before we could arrive in the mountain village of Grimentz, just a couple of train and bus rides away. How, we pondered, could we make the best use of that time? We thought we knew a way.

It was already past 6 p.m. when we stepped off the bus in Argentière and almost immediately began our second climb towards Lac Chéserys. Our plan was to take advantage of a fine weather forecast and perhaps enjoy the Perseid meteor shower, which was due to peak that very night, before ascending to Lac Blanc the following day to finally enjoy the fabulous, famous view that had been denied us by the rain a couple of days earlier. With just a couple more nights left under canvas, we couldn't think of a more beautiful and suitable place to say our final farewell to the hills before slipping into the arms of luxury for a short while.

From Argentière we had over 1000 metres to ascend and less than 3 hours of daylight to do it in, but we knew we had it in us. Settling down for our second night by the gently lapping waters of Lac Chéserys, nestled in precisely the same spot we had rested upon three nights ago, was a near perfect moment. These hills had been our home for the best part of three weeks and in just a couple more nights we would have moved on, but for now there was no more homely spot in the entire world.

Vital Statistics - Day 20
Start: Les Houches
End: Lac Chéserys
Distance Hiked: 6 kilometres
Hiking Time: 3 hours
Height Gain: 1000 metres
Height Loss: 0 metres

Epilogue

Our second morning waking at Lac Chéserys dawned bright and clear. A cold two-hour vigil in the early hours had yielded not a single meteor sighting, at least not for me. Esther had spent ages lying with her head out of the tent, looking at the sky, intermittently exclaiming "there's one, quick", at which point I would hasten out of my sleeping bag to see nothing but stationary stars. But that hadn't really mattered. What had mattered was that we were alone and in the hills together, no longer chasing a goal but simply enjoying the stillness of being high above the madness in the valley below. This morning at least we had nowhere to rush off too. Instead we slowly ate breakfast watching the clouds lift from the awesome peaks and glaciers of the Mont Blanc massif across the valley.

After an hour or so basking in the crisp morning air we made our way a little further up the mountainside to Lac Blanc and "Wow!", it really was just like the guidebook promised. The reality even surpassed our expectations. Glistening azure water reflected the snowy mountains across the valley, with the lake ringed by a rocky bowl which perfectly framed the postcard panorama. It was superb. With the sun shining and warming the rocks, we found ourselves a comfortable perch and settled in for a further 2 hours in order to simply sit and take it all in. Seeing one of Europe's most iconic views reflected double in the still waters of the lake made it feel like we were an integral part of nature's grand canvas, which in a way we were.

Tearing ourselves away, we enjoyed a slow afternoon hike along the Grand Balcon Sud and back down to the Col des Montets, before catching a bus to the village of Vallorcine alongside the French-Swiss border. It was here that we spent our very final night under canvas, on a campsite, before catching the two trains and two buses

170

required to bring us safely into Grimentz, jewel of the Val d'Anniviers, by Saturday afternoon. We found Shirley and Robin's apartment to be the very epitome of perfection when we arrived. Clean, well-appointed and spacious. Everything we had day-dreamed about during the long hot days beneath the sun, trickling greasy suncream into our sweat stained clothes.

Ah, Grimentz! One of Switzerland's most beautiful mountain villages, where sun-blackened wooden houses decorated with red geraniums are set against the backdrop of sweeping green hillsides and snow-capped 4000-metre peaks. This was the valley we had fallen in love with during our motorhome adventure and it was also the place we'd grown to think of as our 'energetic' home, where our energy was always lifted and where we felt more like we belonged than anywhere else on Earth.

During our week-long stay in Val d'Anniviers we reacquainted ourselves with some of our most beloved day hikes. We trekked to the Cabane du Petit Mountet and the Cabane du Moiry, we walked to the top of the Corne du Sorebois, we ran together to the Roc d'Orzival and we also pottered around the village, playing multiple rounds of sunny mini-golf as the long summer evenings slowly closed. Barely a daylight hour went by which didn't see us outside and revelling in the natural beauty all around us. But there was also no doubt that we saved the best for last, waiting until our penultimate day in Switzerland to ascend to the place where the feeling of belonging was more intense, more uplifting, than anywhere else in the valley.

Quite why the summit of the 2906 metre Scex de Marenda had always captivated us so powerfully is hard to say. In terms of scenery it is almost flawless, but then the same can be said of many of our favourite places in the Val d'Anniviers. And as vantage points go for taking in almost the entire valley it is equally perfect, but again it is not unique in this either. What is unique, however, is that every time we have found ourselves approaching the summit cairn, negotiating the narrow ridge which seems to jut out clear above the valley floor, we feel new life flowing into our limbs. Almost nowhere else do we feel quite as energised and connected to everything around us as we do in this magical place.

We approached the summit together, breathing hard and sweating harder as we climbed high above the valley floor to within a whisker of 3000 metres, almost completely exposed as we traversed the final ridge with sheer drops on three sides and panoramic views across the surrounding Swiss Alps. This was a wild place, a place of sparkling azure lakes, pristine white summits, grey-blue tumbling glaciers, lush green fir trees and, perhaps most importantly for us, relatively little evidence of civilisation.

All around us sun-warmed stones seemed to be inviting us to sit, to rest, and marvel at the views on offer, across hundreds of miles of clear Alpine air in every direction. To the north the ridges of the Bernese Alps, of the Jungfrau, Eiger and Mönch, could be clearly picked out against the sky. To the south the Moiry Lake sparkled in the sun, while boulders of ice from the Moiry glacier crowded towards the water's edge. To the east the various 4000 metre summits, for which this particular valley is famous, stood tall above their assorted snowfields. To the west, beyond the ridge we had just ascended, waves of yellowed mountainside, the grass scorched by the heat of summer, rolled away. It was nothing short of magnificent.

Seconds later it was all gone. Vanished. Snuffed out by a previously wispy tendril of cloud that had been fading in and out of existence all morning, but which had chosen this special moment to suddenly inflate and sweep over us. Dense mist now hemmed us in from all sides and anything more than 5 metres away was lost in the grey. Immediately the air had turned cold and with our still sweating bodies losing heat quickly, my instinct was to start downhill sooner rather than later. The last thing I wanted was to get soaked, or even potentially lost, in a mountain storm, no matter how beautiful the climb had been.

"Let's go" I said to Esther. "We've had the view on the way up and I'm getting cold. I can't see this going anywhere soon. We were lucky to get here before it closed in".

"Hang on a moment" Esther replied. "Just five minutes. I have a feeling it might lift". So, we pulled on the few flimsy extra layers we were carrying and waited.

Five minutes came and went and we were still surrounded by mist. The only change was that the wind had picked up as well, pushing the clouds surrounding us quickly across our faces, darkening as they condensed in heavy droplets on our hats and gloves. In response, I had pretty much resigned myself to a sodden and tricky descent.

But then, just as we were about to beat a hasty downhill retreat, a window in the grey appeared. A shaft of sunlight pierced the gloom and left us momentarily warm again, looking up at a patch of blue sky. This first patch of brilliance vanished quickly, lasting just a few seconds, but others soon followed, popping in and out of our world like bubbles of revelation, revealing not only sky but snatches of scenery as well. A portion of mountain here, a chunk of glacier there, a patch of water, a cluster of tiny houses far below. Piece by short-lived piece the amazing view we'd fallen in love with returned and disappeared chaotically. It wasn't a storm that had been on the way after all, just a band of very dense cloud blowing through.

We were holding hands, enjoying the spectacle in companionable silence, when Esther suddenly said "You know, this makes me realise that even when there are clouds in the way, the view is always still there, just waiting to be seen".

"It is beautiful" I agreed, but it was only hours later that the real significance of what Esther had said hit me.

This had been our final day of hiking before leaving the mountains behind. The very next morning we were

173

heading back to Geneva airport, after almost a month in the Alps, living out of rucksacks, sleeping in a tent and making up our plan usually as we went along. There had been dazzling scenery, laughter, new friendships, overwhelming kindness from complete strangers and moments of sheer, unmatched joy. Moments when we had felt nothing short of ecstatic. Yet there had also been some tears, shouting and tension too. Times when we'd tried, and failed, to work out why we were even out here in the first place. But there had always been a reason. It had always been there, we just hadn't always been able to see it.

So, what had we learned from our month in the mountains, if anything? Were there any life lessons waiting to be discovered behind the clouds? I've heard it said that the reason we tell stories is to try and make sense of our lives. I think this is probably true. Yet it is sometimes dangerous to try and tell a story in such a way as to wrap a bow around the ending and imply that there was a simple answer waiting at the end of the rainbow. Life, I've come to find, is rarely so neat and tidy.

Truth is, it would be a long time after our adventure in the mountains ended that we would start to get a handle on what I now consider the most important lesson of all, that many of our choices were still influenced by a need to be seen 'achieving' stuff, but that's not to say there was nothing we took away with us immediately either. We had already realised, prior even to leaving Switzerland for example, that we had set out from the UK with insufficient commitment to our claimed objective, that is to hike through the mountains for a month. We'd thought we'd been committed, but when the going had gotten tough our doubts and anxieties had said otherwise. Commitment, we'd come to accept during the previous month, was really only one side of a coin, the other side being sacrifice. We'd talked about commitment to our hike but we'd never really sat down and weighed up the necessary sacrifices that our commitment would demand of us. A degree of physical discomfort and fatigue we'd anticipated, but difficulties accessing toilets, friction between the two of us, ME challenges, accommodation uncertainties etc. just hadn't been considered. To some extent it is impossible to anticipate every possible challenge that an adventure of this kind can throw up, but we'd anticipated hardly any. Instead we'd bumbled into it wearing rose-tinted glasses and wrapped in a sense of arrogance, and that is probably why, when the going did get tough, we wasted so much energy trying to work out how we might change things. Any future projects or adventures, therefore, would require a lot more consideration regarding what sacrifices we were actually willing to make, and preferably prior to starting out.

Of course, there were also more practical lessons, many of which we had implemented along the way. Refining our equipment to only include the essentials and tailoring our food stock-ups, while trusting to the advertised resupply points to provide what we needed, were some of the most obvious, but in a way these were only superficial trivialities. Our decision-making had also been ludicrously convoluted, taking far longer than it ever should have done in an effort to weigh up all possible options and make sure we didn't miss out on anything, rather than simply listening to our gut instincts.

On a more positive note, however, we also came away from the Alps feeling elated and incredibly grateful at how well our bodies had coped with the stress we'd unexpectedly thrown at them. We'd gone from gorging on dairy-free ice cream to marching uphill in the space of just a few days, yet the adaptations required for us to keep going had been swift and significant. We'd lost weight rapidly, our lungs had seemed to double in size, and our thighs, backs and arms had developed sinews that had kept us hiking long after we should have allowed them to rest. Learning that our bodies could do that for us was a special gift, and in return we'd done our best to feed them as well as we possibly could. Knowing what we now knew about

175

the availability of fresh, vibrant, organic food in the most unexpected places was another wonderful lesson and one which we knew would bring new optimism and trust to any future forays into the wilderness. It was possible to remain plant-based in the mountains after all.

But all of this paled into insignificance compared to the biggest insight of all. The insight that would only strike us months later and only after we'd fallen foul of it countless times again already. Our subconscious need to use our adventures to justify ourselves to the world was a shadow that had hounded us for years before we even noticed it. It seems so obvious now, looking back, but ever since we had set off in a motorhome in 2014 we hadn't been able to give ourselves permission to enjoy ourselves and just be completely grateful for the freedom we had fallen into. Instead of revelling in the spaciousness of not having a house to clean, jobs to go to and a lawn to mow, we had filled the void with arbitrary 'ambitions', feeling compelled to prove we weren't just "bumming around" by always going further, faster and higher than everyone else.

"Just keep walking", "pushing on" and "one more climb" had all been minor manifestations of this trait, as had racing Paddy and trying to make it all the way to Nice despite being several days short on time and the fact that it was hardly a convenient destination given our need to return to Geneva afterwards. Yet the fact that our hike was more than just a holiday in our minds, but was also a medal that we hoped to 'win' and then pin onto our 'CV of life', incurred a deeper cost than a few sore feet and angry voices. You see, during the many moments that we were fatigued but pushed on anyway, driven by our subconscious insecurities, we also forgot to enjoy the moment. We were cracking our own whip, entirely unnecessarily, and if we'd actually listened to our bodies, slowed down and stopped sooner on most days, then we could have had an even more pleasurable experience overall.

Except, of course, it's only a failing if we fail to learn from it. Like I said, it still took us a while after we left the Alps to even notice this trait during which we fell foul of our ambitious egos' many more times, but I think we started to get there in the end. Or at least I hope so. I don't want to sugar-coat things to make the end of this book nice and cuddly, or imply that due to our long walk through the Alps we achieved some sort of Zen-like state of being, where we are fully at one with each other and the world around us, because that would be a load of crap. Truth is, we still 'fall' often. We still try and do too much in order to achieve 'stuff', we still try and push our bodies way beyond their limits and we still enter into projects without fully appreciating the demands they will place on us. The only real difference, in fact, is that now that we have at least started noticing this trait, we are better able to catch ourselves and say "hang on, we're doing it again, aren't we? Why don't we make a different choice?" Sometimes it works, mostly it doesn't, but it's definitely a step in the right direction.

I also have to be careful of myself at this point because I know I have a tendency to focus on heavy, serious things like the 'lessons' above, often at the expense of the fun stuff, and that just wouldn't be a fair way to end this story. I mean, yes, there were many moments when our bodies said "can we stop, please?" and our egos' said "no, we must go faster", and that did lead to negative experiences. But that's not the whole story either, and nor is it what we were smiling at each other about the day that our plane flew out of Geneva.

Most of what we took away from our month in the mountains were happy memories. Memories of the wonderful people we had met, memories of the kindness of strangers, memories of the stunning scenery we had lived surrounded by, memories of feeling immersed in a simpler way of life, and memories of the feeling of freedom we had

177

experienced while sleeping beneath the stars and watching majestic sunsets in splendid isolation.

Thank You

Hello wonderful reader and thank you for making it all the way to the end of *Turn Left At Mont Blanc*, the first book in the Alpine Thru-Hiking series.

I know you could have picked any number of books to read, but you picked this one and for that I am extremely grateful.

I hope that it made you smile and, just maybe, had you day-dreaming of high mountains, snow-covered glaciers and Alpine lakes, some of the finest treasures our planet has to offer.

If so, it would be wonderful if you'd take a few seconds to leave a review on Amazon. Your review is very important and will only take a matter of seconds. Also, if you can, it would be really nice if you could share this book with your friends and family by posting to Facebook and Twitter.

And, if you want to continue the adventure with us, flip to the back of this book to learn about the rest of the books in the Alpine Thru-Hiking series.

Thank you.

Acknowledgements

Writing a book takes time and words, but it also takes a lot of love and support. The adventure I've written about was one that Esther and I undertook together, and it turned out that writing about it was an equally joint project.

I may have been the one banging at a keyboard, meaning all mistakes and typos are my own, but without Esther's steadfast encouragement, unrivalled memory for details and unwavering desire to listen to my ramblings and make gentle suggestions, then it's likely this book would still exist only in my head.

Thank you, I love you.

Dan Colegate 2019

www.estheranddan.com

www.instagram.com/estheranddan

www.facebook.com/estheranddan

180

Photos

1 A view across Lac Blanc towards the Mont Blanc Massif

2 - On the Fenêtre d'Arpette, overlooking the Glacier du Trient

3 - A lone chamois wandering along the Grand Balcon Sud

4 - Camping beneath the Col d'Anterne, overlooking Mont Blanc

5 - Descending from the Col de la Seigne

6 - One of countless marmot chirruping by the trail

7 - Overlooking the Glacier du Moiry in the Val d'Anniviers

8 - Among the clouds on the Scex de Marenda, Val d'Anniviers

9 - Hiking into Les Houches from the summit of La Brévent

These are just a few images from many thousands. For more photos from our adventures, visit our website at **www.estheranddan.com** or our Instagram page **www.instagram.com/estheranddan**

Also By The Author

What Adventures Shall We Have Today?
Travelling From More To Less In Search Of A Simpler Life

You've read one small part of our adventures, now read about the rest! The perfect book for anyone who has ever felt there could be more to life.

Six years ago Dan and Esther were counting down the days until their wedding and the honeymoon of their dreams. Then Dan almost died. Told to say goodbye to each other "just in case" in the early hours of a sleeting January morning, that was the moment when their lives would change forever. Three months later they drove away from their home, their jobs and everything they'd ever known in a second-hand motorhome. Friends and family asked "What do you want to see? Where do you want to go?". All they could say in response was "it's a feeling we're searching for."

At first they planned to travel for a year but as their outlook on life evolved, their priorities changed and they started to get glimpses of 'that feeling', their escape quickly morphed into a lifestyle all of its own.

This is the story of their travels for the past six years. With no plan and no purpose beyond living in the moment, their meandering adventures have taken them over mountains, under the sea, inside of pyramids and across the skies. They've crashed a hot air balloon by the Nile, adopted a dog who surprised them by being pregnant and even became organic farmers for a while, among other things. More than anything, however, they've found themselves confronting their own insecurities and limiting beliefs about how life is supposed to be lived.

187

This is more than a story of two people drifting around Europe, it's about looking at the world through fresh eyes, reassessing what's truly important and embracing the inevitable challenges that life throws up.

Visit **www.estheranddan.com** or Amazon to find out more.

WHAT ADVENTURES SHALL WE HAVE TODAY?

DAN COLEGATE

Just Around The Matterhorn

Lose yourself in the heart of the Alps, in the shadow of Europe's most iconic mountain.

The second book in the Alpine Thru-Hiking series. Three busy years after the adventures in this book, Dan and Esther are eager to set out once more into the wilderness. They decide to try the Tour of the Matterhorn, but with no fixed itinerary or timeframe, they find themselves taking a somewhat different route as they hike and camp higher than they've ever been before.

Having started out determined to "take it easy", they instead find themselves pushing their boundaries across glaciers, precipitous ridges and vertical laddered cliffs while also battling illness and at times being hardly able to eat.

Taking in the entire Tour of the Matterhorn and Tour of Monte Rosa (the second highest mountain in the Alps), the remainder of the Chamonix-to-Zermatt Haute Route and a little of the Tour des Combins, their four week odyssey becomes a deep exploration of the finest scenery the Alps has to offer. With almost 25 vertical kilometres of ascent over 320 kilometres of hiking, surrounded by dozens of famous 4000 metre summits, monumental glaciers and remote mountain valleys, it's an adventure not to be missed.

Visit **www.estheranddan.com** or Amazon to find out more.

JUST AROUND
the
MATTERHORN

Two People
Four Weeks
One Adventure

DAN COLEGATE

Walking Through Paradise
A Magnificent Journey Through Western Europe's Largest Nature Reserve

Book three in the Alpine Thru-Hiking series is a light-hearted, uplifting and inspiring account of Dan and Esther's fifteen day odyssey through the French and Italian Alps, exploring the Vanoise and Gran Paradiso National Parks.

Just five days after their demanding four-week adventure around the Matterhorn, Esther and Dan set out into the wilderness once again. Their goal is simple, to enjoy a peaceful walking holiday in the Alps. However, as usual, the moment their shoes hit the trail their plans go straight out of the window and the adventure takes on a life of its own.

Driven by an inexplicable thirst to always look beyond the next summit, their initially sedate hike from refuge-to-refuge soon becomes an expedition across blizzard-ridden 3000-metre passes, tumultuous boulder fields and snow-packed glaciers, turning each day into a unique pilgrimage through some of the most remote and stunning Alpine scenery they've ever seen.

Sleeping in everything from luxury hotels to snow-covered storm-shelters and abandoned tree houses, their quest to lose themselves in the heart of the Alps becomes far more than a search for nice views and exciting stories. It's about rediscovering the solitude of the hills and the calm of the night sky, miles from civilisation and the chaos of the modern world.

A perfect book for anyone who wants to experience the awe-inspiring magic of Europe's most beautiful wilderness.

Visit **www.estheranddan.com** or Amazon to find out more.

WALKING THROUGH PARADISE

A Magnificent Journey
Through The Heart Of The Alps

DAN COLEGATE